# Football's Seven Best Offenses

**Other books by the author:**

*Football Coach's Guide to Successful Pass Defense*
*Football's Fabulous Forty Defense*
*Complete Book of Triple Option Football*
*Complete Guide to the Fifty Defenses in Football*

# FOOTBALL'S SEVEN BEST OFFENSES

## Jack Olcott

**Parker Publishing Company, Inc.**
**West Nyack, New York**

© 1978, by

PARKER PUBLISHING COMPANY, INC.

West Nyack, N.Y.

**Library of Congress Cataloging in Publication Data**

Olcott, Jack.
  Football's seven best offenses.

  Includes index.
  1.  Football--Offense.  2.  Football coaching.
I.  Title.
GV951.8.O393        796.33'22        78-870
ISBN 0-13-324699-X

Printed in the United States of America

# What This Book Will Do For You

Now you can select an offense to fit your players. Football's seven best offenses are described and diagrammed in detail along with a suggested type of football player who best fits into each particular style of offense.

Whether you are looking for a complete offense or just a few new offensive plays to add to your attack, this book will give you the step-by-step coaching points of how to put more scoring punch into your attack.

The purpose of this book is to give you a complete view of seven of football's best offensive attacks, and how to establish a sound and effective manner of applying the correct concepts to make each offense a winner. Thus, this book shows you how to apply a particular offense and how to teach it to each member of the team.

This guide features the most modern high-scoring, high-powered, and wide-open football formations. *Football's Seven Best Offenses* offers all of the latest fundamentals and techniques, from the basics to the most intricate and sophisticated teaching methods.

Each chapter gives you the particular details that show how to block for the total passing game, how to block today's multiple-shifting defenses, and how to block the most successful goal line defenses.

The offensive fundamentals, plays, and teaching techniques found in this book have been collected during the author's twenty years of coaching on both the high school and college levels. Most of this information was gathered via visits to various schools, clinics, film studies, discussions, staff meetings, reading, and extensive research into the most successful offensive formations.

This is a complete book about seven styles of offensive attacks, and it explains these explosive attacks in a simple, logical, and direct manner. Thus, I explain how to execute each formation with the most up-to-date teaching techniques. All of the offensive coaching points in each chapter may be applied to any offense you may select.

This book is not only important from the offensive point of view, but is also a must for the defensive-minded coach. Now as the defender you can read about the strong points of each attack you must face. The more you understand about an offense, the more successful you may be when facing the offense.

This book describes how to control the football game. One of these offenses, series, or even a particular play may force the defense to readjust its basic defensive front or perimeter line of defense. Now the offense has gained the initiative, because it has dictated the defense to adjust to a particular offensive "look." Now the offense has gained the upper hand, and the offense can now control the tempo of the game.

This book enables you to select a particular series or even a specific play which you may easily adapt to your basic offense. With this winning offensive combination, you may keep the defense off balance so it will never regain its composure.

Each offensive formation, play, and every individual coaching point has been described and diagrammed in detail. This offensive book has been written from a "how-to-do-it" approach. Complete backfield play, line blocking rules, and strategic coaching points make this a unique book for all football coaches.

**Jack Olcott**

# CONTENTS

**Contents**

# Football's Seven Best Offenses

# 1

# THE WING-T OFFENSE

## How the Wing-T Formation Will Help You to Win

Influence blocking and the high priority placed upon finessing or faking the defender away from the point of attack, rather than over-powering the defender with a hard-nosed double team block, is one reason why many coaches adopt the Wing-T offense. The Wing T is based upon execution, speed, and deception rather than size and power. Many coaches whose personnel lends itself to the smaller, quicker and more disciplined players gain quick success with this offense. The more disciplined player realizes that it may take time to exploit the sequential football philosophy; but once a defensive weakness is found, the Wing-T offense will quickly take advantage of this weakness.

Offensive motion and quick backfield shifts are important facets of this attack. Once the basic attack has been displayed, the counter, misdirection, and bootleg plays help to spotlight the Wing T as one of football's most explosive offensive attacks.

15

## The Advantages of the Wing-T Offense

1. The Wing-T attack features sequential football. Thus, a particular successful play helps to set up a similar offensive run or pass play. The play sequence may resemble a specific backfield action, line blocking influence assignment, or a combination of both.

2. This attack minimizes pursuit with misdirection of both backfield and offensive linemen flow.

3. The sequential flow of the offensive linemen and backs helps to take advantage of a particular move or reaction of an isolated defender or group of defenders.

4. The simple Wing-T alignment helps to outflank many of the defensive fronts. This means the outside offensive blockers often have outside-in blocking angles on the wide defenders.

5. Offensive shifting and motion help to create an advantageous offensive ratio over the defense at the point of the attack. These two basic offensive adjustments help the offense to out-flank the defense.

6. The Wing-T shift eliminates the true Monster Defense, because it forces the Monster to run all the way across the formation following a quick shift. This is an impossible assignment for the Monster man.

7. The backfield shift and motion make it impossible for the defense to employ a flip-flop defense. This means the left end must only play a left end position and will not be able to take a predetermined strong or weakside defensive alignment.

8. The counters, reverses, and bootlegs take advantage of the fast-pursuing defenders.

9. The counters and the cross-counter action of the offense hold up the revolving and rotating secondary members as well as the regular pursuing defensive assignments.

10. The mesmerizing effects of the pulling guards in the Wing-T offense set up the "sucker play" as a consistent Wing-T gainer. This play is a give to the dive man directly over the vacated offensive area from where the offensive guard has just pulled. This makes the naked dive go without the aid of the offensive guard's block; it is predicated, rather, upon the linebackers' key of reacting or going in the same direction as the pulling guard.

11. The normal wingback's alignment often discourages a defensive leveling of the secondary's technique to the strong side with the split end's wide threat to the opposite side of the formation.

12. The Wing T forces most teams to use an eight man front defense to stop the Wing T's running attack.

13. This attack has the ability to mirror its offensive plays with the slotback assigned to the tight end's blocking or pass receiving assignments.

14. The continual threat of the misdirection advantage forces the often frustrated individual defender to accept the philosophy, "I am wrong if I do react, and I am wrong if I don't react!"

## Requirements for the Wing-T Personnel

*Quarterback*—The quarterback should be a good ball handler. He must be a good play action and roll-out passer, as this offense underlines the importance of the bootleg pass on most of its basic plays. The quarterback must be cool and disciplined. He must learn to take his time and calculate each maneuver to set up his ultimate game plan.

*Fullback*—Should be selected primarily for his faking and blocking ability. Most of his running plays tend to make the runner more effective rather than the runner making the play a consistent threat. The misdirection, counters, and bootleg maneuvers help to set up the fullback as a basic Wing-T scoring threat.

*Tailback*—Primarily he is a running threat, but because of the shifts, he should also be a capable blocker and receiver. Speed and quickness are important assets for this ball carrier.

*Wingback*—Must be able to block and catch the ball. He should also be an experienced runner, not only on reverses and counters, but from a set position because of the Wing-T quick shifts.

*Split End*—This wide receiver should be a good gamebreaking threat. He should have speed and the ability to make the big catch.

*Tight End*—The tight end should be a blocker first and a pass receiver second. Good size helps the tight end's inside blocking assignments versus the larger interior defenders.

*Tackle*—Should be a good, strong shoulder blocker who can execute the one-on-one block as well as the cut-off and double team blocks.

*Guards*—Must be quick-pulling blockers who have the ability to trap the defender and lead the ball carrier on sweeps and off tackle plays. The guards must be coachable and be able to make the key bootleg as well as the counter block at the point of the attack.

*Center*—The pivot man must be quick enough to block the defensive odd middle guard and strong enough to block back on the even backside defender. The center must be the first blocker across the line and must be a solid pass blocker.

The basic philosophy of the Wing-T attack is to establish the fullback off tackle play as a consistent ground gainer. One of the finest blocking adjustments against both the Oklahoma (52) and the Split Forty (44) defenses is to kick out the #3 defender with the frontside guard while blocking down with the frontside offensive tackle and end.

Diagram 1-1 illustrates the frontside guard's kick-out block to the tight end's side versus the 52 Defense. The wingback has the key influence block on the defensive #3 man. The #3 defender has to step toward or at least be influenced by the wingback's down-blocking threat. Both the offensive end and tackle have fine angles on their assigned defenders, and the frontside guard has a fine inside-out angle on the #3 defender.

The fullback belly play to the wingback's side is also a very successful maneuver against the Split Forty (44) Defense. Against this defense, the tight end blocks down and helps to block the scrapping frontside inside linebacker. Diagram 1-2 points out how the offensive end and tackle seal off the interior defenders, which opens up the offensive crease that was started by the frontside guard's trap block on the #3 defender. The center and backside offensive guard are assigned to pick off the interior split linebackers. The reason the guard has such an easy kick-out block versus the #3 defender is because the defender is mainly responsible for containing the quarterback's roll-out pass or run play. The #4 defender is frozen by the very nature of his flat assignment.

Once the offensive sweep (featuring the fake to the fullback over

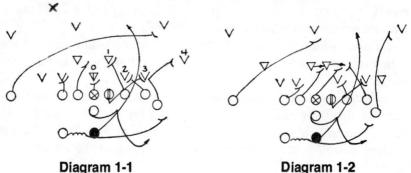

**Diagram 1-1**                              **Diagram 1-2**

the center) has been established as a consistent gainer (Diagram 1-3), coaches of the Wing T like to come back and run the sucker play. Since the inside linebackers realize they must key the pulling guards and pursue the wide sweep threat, the Wing T uses the influence of the sucker play to take advantage of the overly eager pursuing linebackers.

## Fullback Sucker Dive Versus 52 Defense

As Diagram 1-4 illustrates, the frontside left linebacker (circled) is the man the offense is influencing. This defender normally is in such a rush to scallop in his pursuit course to stop the sweep that he usually ignores the fullback's quick dive. The #2 defender is also influenced to react to the potential sweep, as the tight end is instructed to use an outside quick influence slam block. This forces the defensive tackle (#2) to react normally and fight against the outside pressure block of the tight end's apparent outside drive block. This

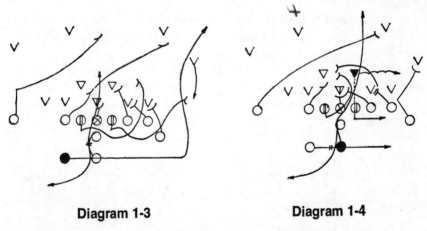

Diagram 1-3                              Diagram 1-4

influence block normally occupies the #2 defender long enough to enable the fullback to successfully make his dive cut. The frontside tackle drives down on the #0 defender and completes the double team block with the center as the post man. The backside guard is coached to pull (emulating his sweep-blocking assignment) and turn upfield, just beyond the double team block on the nose guard, and seal off the backside linebacker's pursuit. The backside tackle also fires out to block the backside linebacker to insure against a possible blitz by this defender.

## Fullback Sucker Dive Against the 44 Defense

Against the 44 Defense, the frontside linebacker (circled) is influenced away from the point of attack by the pulling frontside guard and the apparent threat of the Wing-T sweep.

In Diagram 1-5 the center blocks back on the defensive tackle and the backside guard folds around the center's block and is taught to cut off the backside linebacker. The Wing T's "touchdown makers" (downfield blockers) are assigned to block the three deep secondary defenders.

## Influencing the Outside Linebacker (Eight Man Front)

Once the Wing-T Offense has established the outside attack, the 44 or 62 linebacker will try to cover the flat versus the belly pass; the quarterback is then instructed to attack the area vacated by this defender.

Diagram 1-6 features the successful belly pass against a three deep secondary. Since the outside linebacker (circled) must cover the outside flat, the curl pass is open.

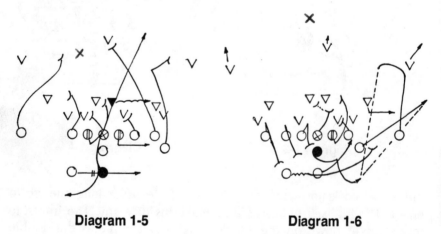

Diagram 1-5                          Diagram 1-6

If the outside linebacker does not cover the slotback in the flat, he must cover the curl zone. Therefore, the Wing-T attack takes advantage of the #3 defender's assignment and hands the ball off on a fullback belly play (Diagram 1-7). The defensive end (#4) must contain the possible option pitch-out to the trailing halfback, coupled with the possible roll-out run by the quarterback. This holds the #4 defender to defend against the outside offensive threat. The fullback therefore has a large hole to make his downfield break. The fold block of the frontside guard and tackle helps to seal off the interior #1 and #2 defenders. The center is coached to take a step to the playside to insure against a possible straight-ahead blitz by the frontside #1 man.

When the defensive end is assigned to take the fullback, the quarterback merely fakes the ball to the bellying fullback and keeps the ball himself. The quarterback is then escorted downfield by the backside halfback and has two potential downfield blockers, the split end and slotback, who were previously assigned pass routes to the frontside (Diagram 1-8).

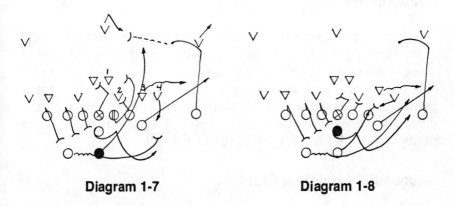

Diagram 1-7                            Diagram 1-8

## Wing-T Blocking Techniques

As stated previously in the advantages of the Wing T, this offense uses a great deal of influence or finesse blocking and faking. These influence or finesse techniques often take precedence over the one-on-one shoulder blocks or the powerful double team blocking techniques. The pulling linemen and the motion and counter patterns by the offensive backs help to set up the bewildered defenders for quick shoulder or influence blocks.

## The Shoulder Block

The shoulder block is the Wing T's basic block. A quick fire-out and an explosive shoulder into the defensive target helps to open up the offensive holes. The blocker explodes into the defender using his shoulder as the striking area. The blocker's head and shoulder combine to employ a squeezing effect on the defender. On contact, the head is up and the blocker's tail must be down. The blocker is coached to use short, powerful, small steps. The knees must be bent so the blocker can explode into the defender by rolling and extending his hips into the target. Thus, the explosion is made by bringing the blocker's hands, elbows, and hips up and through the defender. The follow-through is coached by continually encouraging the blocker to keep his head up, display short, wide-chopping feet, and have an all-out aggressive desire to stay with the defender until the whistle blows.

## Influence Blocking of the Wing T

Influence blocking allows the offensive attack to take advantage of the defender's normal defensive reaction to a fake or influenced block or offensive action. This action may consist of a false pull by an offensive guard, a particular fake by one of the backs, or wingback motion. Any one of the above techniques may have a "pull" on the defender and influence him to leave his primary defensive position—without actually blocking this defender.

## Successful Influence Blocking

The most successful influence blocking attack can only be consistent when the offense has established a particular bread-and-butter play; i.e., a definite offensive threat. Once this play has been established, you must observe that the defender has reacted to this offensive play in a particular manner. This defender's reaction may be seen during a scouting trip, a film exchange, or previously during the actual game.

## The Double Tight Wing T

The Wing T featuring two tight ends is an excellent formation versus the Split Forty or 44 Defense, because this defense ends up in a gap eight charge. The Wing-T formation thus creates nine gaps, and the defense is weakened because it cannot cover nine gaps with only, an eight man front! This means the double tight-wingback offense has minimized the number of defensive stunts. Therefore, the Wing-T Formation dictates what the defense can do (Diagram 1-9).

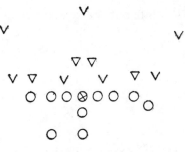

**Diagram 1-9**

Since the Split Forty Defense is a balanced defense, the tight or medium wingback adjustment gives the offense an overbalanced look prior to the snap of the ball.

## The Importance of the Wing-T Sweeps

The sweep action of the Wing T is an important facet of the total picture of the Wing T's formation. These wide maneuvers force the defensive personnel to pursue from sideline to sideline. Once this attack has established the threat of the sweep, all of the other sequences of plays begin to take advantage of the overpursuing defenders. Now the offense may run their traps, counters, reverses, and bootleg plays against the defense. In turn, these plays help the offense to return to attacking the defensive perimeter with the sweeps.

## Unbalanced Wing-T Sweep

The unbalanced line gives the Wing T a unique "look" for the defense. This surprise offensive formation opens up new avenues of thought for the Wing-T offensive strategist.

A brief view of a sweep from the right end over (REO) formation with a slot versus an unadjusted defense would look like Diagram 1-10.

The Wing-T sweep versus the straight Oklahoma Defense would double team the defensive end with the slotback and end, and the ball carrier would turn the corner with both guards clearing the way (Diagram 1-10).

If a 52 Defense decides to overshift a man toward the strong side of the offensive formation, the Wing-T sweep still looks good with the offensive line's blocking-back assignments. The two guards still turn the corner to pave the way for the sweep, as illustrated in Diagram

1-10. Diagram 1-11 points out the sweep versus the 52's overshifted defensive alignment.

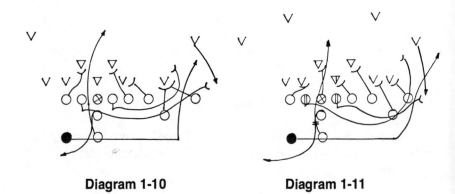

**Diagram 1-10**                          **Diagram 1-11**

*Coaching Point:* The blockers must cut off all defensive penetration along the line of scrimmage. Any defensive penetration will minimize the success of the Wing T's sweeping attack.

The Wing-T Teen Sweep illustrated in Diagram 1-12 is a two-pronged offensive weapon that threatens the defensive interior and the corner. The Teen Sweep linemen's blocking rules are as follows:

| | |
|---|---|
| Split End | — Crack back on first inside defender. |
| Slotback | — Block inside—cut off penetration. |
| Frontside Tackle | — Block down. |
| Frontside Guard | — Pull two yards deep and kick out the first defender outside of the split end's block. |
| Center | — Over, reach to the frontside. |
| Backside Guard | — Pull one yard deep and seal to the inside just beyond the slotback's block. |
| Backside Tackle | — Crossfield (shallow) |
| Backside End | — Deep middle (shallow) |

## The Influence of the F-Sweep

The F-Sweep (Diagram 1-13) designates the fullback to lead the sweep and block the #4 defender. The offensive influence of this maneuver is to have the offensive guards pull in the opposite direc-

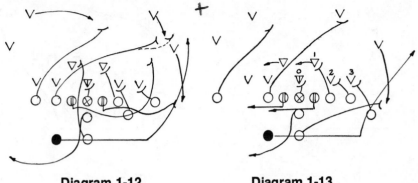

Diagram 1-12          Diagram 1-13

tion of the point of attack. This play is designed with the Oklahoma (52) Defense in mind. Most inside Oklahoma linebackers are taught to key the offensive guards and scallop in the direction of their pulling techniques.

The frontside offensive tackle, end, and wingback are coached to block back on their respective defensive assignments. The frontside offensive tackle is taught to step to his inside and pick off either linebacker.

## The Wing T's Multiple Sweeps

The Wing T enables the wing and the tight end to double team the defensive end. This enables both of the guards to pull around the corner and lead the halfback hand-off Teen Sweep. The fullback dive up the middle helps to hold the inside 52 linebackers, with the frontside (left) tackle blocking down on the frontside defensive tackle (Diagram 1-14).

The bootleg action by the quarterback helps to set up both the bootleg run and the bootleg pass by the quarterback. This counter action by the quarterback, wingback, or set halfback helps to hold the defense for the consistent counter attack of the Wing-T Offense (Diagram 1-14).

Diagram 1-15 illustrates the Wing F (fullback) Sweep. The fullback helps to lead this sweep versus the 62 Defense with the lead halfback blocking at the point of attack on the defensive #3 man. The backside guard pulls and kicks out on the frontside-containing #4 man. All of the frontside offensive linemen block one on one, with the offensive end posting the #3 defender to set up the double team block with the halfback as the drive man. The tackle blocks #2 with

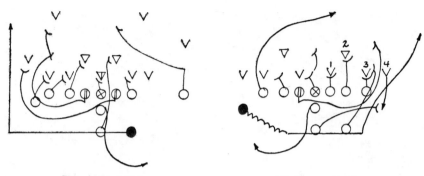

Diagram 1-14                    Diagram 1-15

the frontside guard blocking #1. The center and backside tackle block back on their respective defenders. The backside end blocks the deep middle one third area. After the hand-off, the quarterback continues to fake his bootleg action away from the sweep (Diagram 1-15).

The Power Pitch Sweep featured in Diagram 1-16 pictures both guards, the quarterback, fullback, and frontside halfback leading the Power Sweep. The frontside end blocks back on the #2 man and the frontside tackle blocks back on the #1 defender. The quarterback uses a reverse pivot, leads the short-motioning slotback with a soft, hanging pitch, then runs a shallow path down the line of scrimmage to get out in front of the sweeping slotback (ball carrier).

The halfback-to-halfback reverse helps to cut down the quick-pursuing defense. The counter action holds some defenders long enough to set them up for a key block or to take them out of their normal quick-pursuit route.

Diagram 1-17 demonstrates how the quarterback opens up, makes a quick fake to the fullback, and hands the ball off to the left halfback. The halfback then begins to sweep to his right and slips the ball off to the reversing slotback on a hidden inside hand-off. The left halfback keeps faking his sweep right, while the slotback carries the ball in the opposite direction. The slotback is coached to follow his pulling right guard. As soon as the pulling guard traps the defensive #3 man, the ball carrier is coached to cut upfield off the butt of the pulling guard's kick-out block. The halfback-to-slotback reverse actually turns up inside the defensive end off the double team block on the #2 defender by the posting offensive left tackle and drive-blocking left end. The frontside guard and center's one-on-one blocks are made easier via the holding counter action of the halfback-to-halfback reverse.

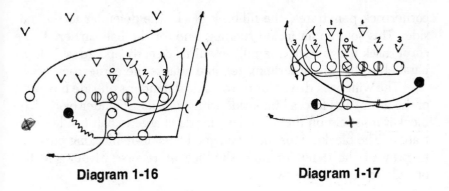

| Diagram 1-16 | Diagram 1-17 |

## Wing-T Fullback Sweep

The Wing T's Fullback Sweep (Diagram 1-18) features the fullback leading the sweep as the lead blocker. The backfield techniques are taught in the following manner:

The quarterback is taught to use a reverse pivot and set his course straight backward, directly at the fullback's original position. The quarterback's path is perpendicular to the line of scrimmage, and he hands the ball off with his right hand (on sweep left). It is up to the quarterback to adjust his second step to make a smooth hand-off to the ball carrier.

The ball carrier is taught to sprint parallel to the line of scrimmage, setting his course directly through the fullback's original position. The ball carrier must raise his inside elbow to accept the ball. Once the ball carrier has accepted the ball, he must check the blocking at the corner (point of attack), then adjust his cut according to the block pattern.

The fullback must sprint parallel to the line of scrimmage. If the

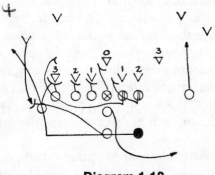

Diagram 1-18

cornerback penetrates, the fullback blocks the defender to the out-side. This sets up an inside running lane for the ball carrier. If the cornerback hangs back, the fullback turns directly upfield (shoulders parallel to the line of scrimmage), and attacks the cornerback.

The wingback drives for the outside defender's outside hip (crest of the ilium) and forces him inside with an inside shoulder block. The blocker must cut off the defender's inside charge to halt inside pene-tration. The blocker must maintain good outside-in blocking pressure to prevent the defender from shuffling or reverse pivoting to the outside to contain the sweep.

## Blocking the Fullback Sweep

The blocking on the F-Sweep (Diagram 1-18) features a double team block by the left end and the wingback on the #3 defender. This double team block is selected whenever the offense comes up against a big, strong, aggressive defender who is too difficult for the wingback to block one-on-one. The frontside tackle, guard, and the center are assigned to cut off the defender who lines up on their outside shoul-der. The backside guard is taught to pull, turn the corner, and look for the first defender to show from the inside. This successful seal block on the backside pulling guard enables the ball carrier to turn up inside the fullback's turn-out block on the #4 defender. The backside tackle also pulls to his inside and is assigned to cut off the pursuit of the backside #1 defender. The split end runs a normal fly pattern.

## Wing-T Sweep's Backfield Techniques

The quarterback is coached to turn out toward the hole and make a quick empty-hand fake to the diving fullback. It is the quarterback's responsibility to clear the fullback. The quarterback must adjust his second step to make the hand-off to the ball carrier.

*Coaching Point:* The quarterback should strike a course perpen-dicular to the line of scrimmage, directly at the original position of the fullback. If the quarterback attempts to step on an angle toward the potential ball carrier, there is a strong possibility that he will under-shoot the halfback, and a fumble or broken play will result in this improper route.

The ball carrier is coached to sprint directly over the original position of the fullback. The ball carrier should continue parallel to the line of scrimmage and raise his inside elbow to accept the ball from the quarterback. He should continue his course until he checks the block on the defensive corner. Then he should make his cut for daylight.

The fullback should set a course for the inside foot of the backside offensive guard, fake a dive by accepting a fake hand-off with his inside elbow up, and be ready to be tackled. A good fake by the diveback holds the linebackers long enough to set them up for the proper offensive blocks.

The wingback's or slotback's blocking is predicated upon this rule (Diagram 1-19).

## Fullback Trap Versus 52 Defense

The Fullback Trap is a basic Wing-T play that helps to set up the sweep and the bootleg plays. The quarterback is responsible for clearing the fullback and making an accurate and safe hand-off. The fullback receives the ball with his inside elbow up and sets his course following the path of the pulling backside guard. The backside guard is coached to trap the first defender to show outside of the frontside offensive guard's block. The frontside tackle sets #2 and then turns out on the #3 defender. The wingback has a key block on the frontside inside linebacker (Diagram 1-20).

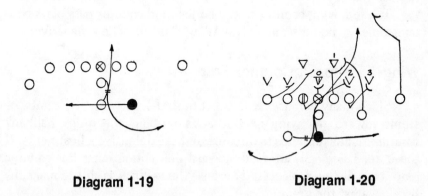

Diagram 1-19                            Diagram 1-20

## Fullback Trap Versus 44 Defense

Against the 44 or Split Forty Defense, many Wing-T offensive units will switch their offensive tackles to guards and their offensive guards to tackles. The coaching point behind this strategic adjustment is that the bigger offensive tackle playing in a guard position is more evenly matched against the normally big defensive tackle playing on his outside shoulder. The offensive guard takes the offensive tackle's normal position and pulls and traps as in his previous assignment against the 52 Defense.

Therefore, the Fullback Trap against the 44 Defense would look like Diagram 1-21. The Fullback Trap becomes a "tackle-like" trap, with the trapper trapping the first defender to show outside of the offensive guard's block. The backside "guard's position" (actually the offensive tackle in the normal guard's position), center, and frontside guard all have excellent blocking angles on their assigned defenders. The offensive frontside "tackle's position" influences the #2 defender and then turns out on the first defender to his outside. The slotback blocks down on the first inside linebacker (Diagram 1-21).

## The Wing T's Counter Attack

The importance of the Wing T's counter play has been previously discussed in this chapter. All of the sequences of Wing-T plays help set up one another. The main reason for the success of the Wing T throughout its many years has been its power to hold the defenders in their original positions, because of continual threat of the counter and reverse plays.

The following counter trap, bootleg, and counter pass plays contain some of the most important Wing-T misdirection maneuvers.

## Wing-T Halfback Counter Trap

Since many defenses will direct their defensive slants, stunts, or stems toward the wing or slotback's motion, the quick halfback counter maneuver helps to discourage these defensive adjustments. If these defensive calls are made toward the motion man, this counter play is usually most successful because the halfback is able to make his break against the grain.

Diagram 1-22 depicts the Halfback Counter Trap versus a Split Forty (44) Defense. The quarterback uses his reverse pivot in the direction of the fullback's belly path and hands the ball off to the halfback with his inside hand. The ball handler is coached to continue on his roll-out course away from the halfback's path. The three in-

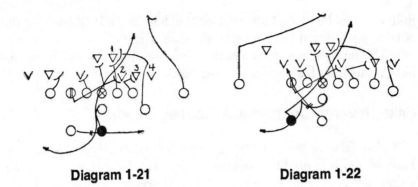

**Diagram 1-21**                         **Diagram 1-22**

terior offensive linemen block away from the hole, and the trapper
traps the first defender to show outside of the offensive guard's normal position. The influence block helps to set up the trap. The offensive end blocks down to the inside and helps to open up the trap hole
by double teaming the frontside inside 44 linebacker at the point of
attack.

The specific timing of this play is predicated upon the ball carrier
taking a quick set step with his outside foot to allow the fullback to
pass by. Then the ball carrier is taught to cut directly off the fullback's
tail and up inside the trapper's block. The fullback's course must take
him just to the outside of the trapper's path so he can avoid colliding
with the trapper.

## Halfback Counter Trap Backfield's Techniques

The quarterback reverses out and chops short his second step to
give the ball off to the countering halfback. The hand-off is made with
the right hand (to the left halfback), and the quarterback is instructed
to roll away from the point of the attack, running his normal bootleg
fake action.

The ball carrier must take a quick set step to his left in order to
allow the fullback to clear his path. Then the ball carrier must set a
course for the outside hip of the center. The ball carrier should lift up
his inside elbow and check the block of the pulling backside tackle.
Against the Split Forty Defense (Diagram 1-22), the ball carrier
should cut off the hip of the pulling tackle, favoring the double team
block on the frontside inside linebacker.

The faking offensive fullback is assigned to make a good fake and
strike a course for the outside hip of the offensive backside guard. The

fullback must be ready to help block the defender if he is favoring the outside shoulder of the backside offensive guard.

The motion back runs a path behind the fullback and turns upfield, emulating his regular bootleg block.

## Fake Reverse-Quarterback Bootleg Pass

The fake reverse action by the offensive wingback and set halfback helps to hold the defensive secondary long enough to spring either the wingback free into the flat or to present an opening for the dragging left tight end. The inside linebackers not only must read reverse halfback-to-halfback action, but they must also check the pull of the backside guard and the bootleg action of the quarterback. The added quarterback's pass or run choice minimizes the pass defense assignment normally expected by the two 52 defensive linebackers.

The quarterback is instructed to open up and turn out toward the point of the attack, using the same steps as assigned on the fullback sweep play. After the fake to the set right halfback, the quarterback is coached to take three slow steps, hiding the ball on his outside hip. After the third step, the quarterback is taught to sprint to the outside and execute his pass or run option.

The passer's first choice is the wingback's flat route. This is a deceptive pass pattern since the wingback's route is hidden a great deal by his behind-the-line fake. Target number two is the left tight end's drag pattern. Because of the reverse action, the third choice (split end running a flag route) is often open because of the key breaking halfback-to-halfback reverse action (Diagram 1-23).

This pass is only used in specific areas on the field. Its success is based upon deception, and it is only used a few times during the season. Yet, once this play has been used, it helps the reverse play to go because the defensive secondary's rotation is slowed by the quarterback's pass or run option.

## Bootleg Fullback Pass

Since many defensive secondaries employ a man-to-man defense to help adjust to the Wing T's shifts and motions, the Bootleg Fullback Pass (Diagram 1-24) helps to take advantage of this secondary alignment. This pass is also a consistent gainer against the three deep (eight man front) and Monster defenses.

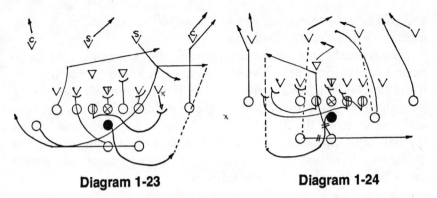

Diagram 1-23                           Diagram 1-24

Blocking assignments for the Bootleg Fullback Pass are as follows:

| Frontside End | — Run a flag pattern. |
|---|---|
| Frontside Tackle | — Gap, over. |
| Frontside Guard | — Pull, seal off penetration. |
| Center | — Over, backside. |
| Backside Tackle | — Pull, block the first defender inside. |
| Backside Guard | — Pull, block the man outside the frontside guard's block. |

*Coaching Point (Backside Guard)*: The backside guard must pull flat and allow the fullback to clear. He then must gain depth and check the first defender to show outside of the frontside guard's block. If no one shows, he should help out the guard.

The quarterback fakes to both the fullback and the left halfback, and bootlegs to the split end's side. He checks the defensive left halfback, as this defender may become a free safety if his key goes away. The primary receiver is the fullback, and the secondary receiver is the curling slotback. In the event that both of these potential receivers are covered, the quarterback should execute his third option and run the ball.

## Wing-T Counter Pass

One of the most consistent passes off the Wing-T attack is the Counter Pass to the fullback in the flat. This pass is most successful against the man-to-man, three deep, locked-in secondary, or away from the Fifty Monster Defense.

Against the man-to-man pass defense, Diagram 1-25 demonstrates how the fullback is able to slip out unnoticed into the flat, with the right halfback's counter fake holding the left safety long enough to work the fullback free. If the #4 defender does not rush and tries to cover the flat (dotted line), the quarterback simply puts the ball away and runs because there is no defender to contain the quarterback's roll-out route. If the #3 defender rushes, the passer drops the quick pass off to the fullback.

Against the Monster Defense, the defensive deep back is responsible to cover the deep outside, allowing the fullback to become a free receiver as seen in Diagram 1-25.

When the defense uses a three deep, locked-in pass defense and an eight man front 62 Defense, the deep safety is unable to cover both the split end's flag cut and the fullback's flat cut. (Diagram 1-26). Now the quarterback must be a little quicker with his release if both the #3 and #4 men rush. The counter action of the right offensive halfback holds the outside-containing #4 man, and the fullback works free behind the #4 defender's back.

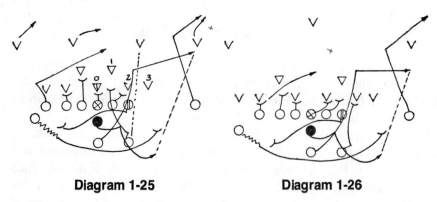

Diagram 1-25                     Diagram 1-26

## Wing-T Bootleg Pass to the Tight End

The bootleg pass is a pass that holds the quick-revolving defensive deep secondary from over-committing. The motion by the wingback makes the secondary move mentally toward the motion man. The quarterback fakes the sweep to the wingback and follows the path of the two pulling guards in the opposite direction, toward the tight end. At the last moment, the quarterback throws a deep flag pass to the tight end against a leaning, countering, and sometimes confused deep secondary (Diagram 1-27).

## Wing-T Bootleg Throwback Pass

Another bootleg pass that has been successful for the Wing-T offense is the Bootleg Throwback Pass. There is an unlimited variety of throwback passes from the bootleg action, and Diagram 1-28 shows one solid throwback pass. The quarterback fakes the sweep to the right halfback and begins to follow his pulling guard toward the tight end's side. Then he pulls up and throws back to the faking right halfback. Normally the right halfback is free because the secondary begins to re-revolve toward the apparent bootleg pass. The split end's deep cut runs off the outside defensive deep back, and the right halfback catches the pass with a great deal of clear territory in front of him.

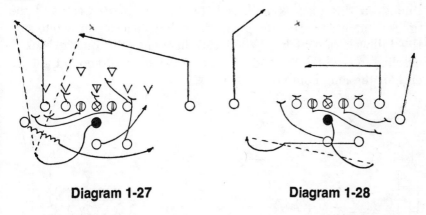

Diagram 1-27                              Diagram 1-28

## The Screen's Counter Action

Another excellent counter play is the Throwback Screen Pass. This pass also helps to limit the defender's pursuit. The Throwback Screen is a combination play-action and screen pass.

## Wing Throwback Screen

The play action and quarterback roll-out away from the direction of the screen pass makes this pass a potential long gainer.

The wingback sets up as if he is going to pass block, then runs behind the line of scrimmage, all the way across the formation. He is taught to set up ten yards outside of the split tackle's original position. The frontside tackle, guard, and center fire out, hit their assigned defenders, and set up a screen to protect the wingback.

A good belly fake must be executed to hold the defenders and time the wingback's screen route. The passer is coached to hit the receiver in the numbers with a bullet pass. If any defender shows between the passer and the potential screen receiver, the quarterback is instructed to either pass to a secondary receiver or run the ball (Diagram 1-29).

## The Wing-T Belly Flag Pass

The strong fullback fake helps to hold the defensive linebackers and allows the quarterback to hit the open receiver. The correct timing on this play-action fake between the quarterback and the fullback often draws the deep pass defenders up a step or two to stop the fullback belly fake. When this happens, the quarterback is coached to read the frontside deep pass defender and go to the tight end for the long bomb (Diagram 1-30).

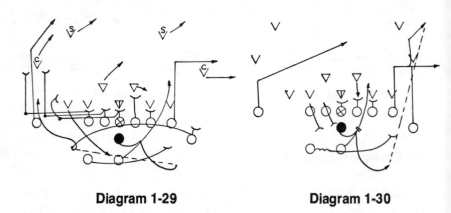

Diagram 1-29                              Diagram 1-30

## Drop-Back and Pull-Up Passes

The Drop-Back Double Curl and the Sprint-Out Pull-Up Seam Pass are two passes that give the Wing-T attack many more passing possibilities.

## Drop-Back Double Curl Pass

The Drop-Back Double Curl (Diagram 1-31) is a balanced pass that can be thrown against any defense. The curling receivers are coached to curl into the secondary seams and slide away from any pass defending linebackers. The straight drop-back pass forces the defensive secondary to make a call to revolve or rotate in a particular manner. The tight end curl is the passer's first priority versus the 52 Monster Defense. Normally, the right defensive inside linebacker will overrun (to the outside) the tight end's curl pattern.

## Sprint-Out Pull-Up Seam Pass

The Seam Pass, as illustrated in Diagram 1-32, teaches the tight end to run a seam between the deep secondary defenders and get open for a throwback pass. The quarterback sprints back and pulls up behind his left offensive guard. The apparent sprint-out action by the quarterback often causes the defensive secondary to revolve in the quarterback's (apparent) sprint-out direction.

Thus, the tight end finds the open seam between the left safety-man and the left cornerback.

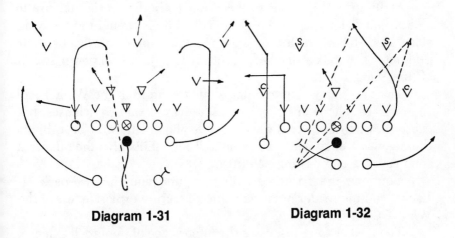

Diagram 1-31                    Diagram 1-32

## Wing-T's Shifting Advantages

Another important phase of the Wing T's attack is the advantageous effect of the quick shift. In a flash, the Wing T has the potential to shift from the Wing T to the Slot Formation (Diagram 1-33), or from the Slot Formation to the Wing-T Formation (Diagram 1-34).

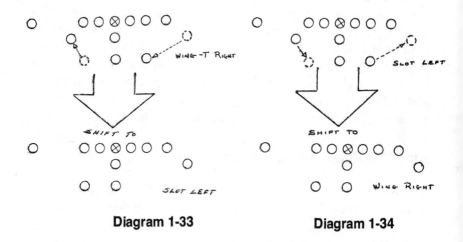

Diagram 1-33                                    Diagram 1-34

The shift from the Wing T to the Slot forces a 52 (Oklahoma) Defense to shift quickly into a double corner defense. As seen in Diagram 1-33, this shift forces the 52 Defense to do something they do not want to do.

Shifting from the Slot to the Wing T also forces the defense to shift from a defense against a slot to adjust their strength to the wing side. This shifting of the defense must be done quickly, or their perimeter may be out-flanked, resulting in a successful power sweep off the Wing T's attack.

You may enjoy diagramming shifts to and from the Wing T and the many problems this offensive shift gives to various defenses, because the offense dictates the defensive alignment or, at best, limits the defensive alignments and stunts. These shifts give the offense a solid running and passing potential.

Combine the backfield shifts, motion, and the two-back "I-Look," and the reader has a view into the future explosiveness of the Wing-T Offense.

The next chapter discusses the importance of the Pro-T Offense. The advantages of the Pro Sweep, the Outside Veer, the Triple Option's blocking techniques, the Quick Pitch, the quarterback's passing reads, how to attack three and four deep secondaries, and the many facets of the Draw Play are described and illustrated.

# 2

# THE PRO-T ATTACK

## How the Pro-T Formation Will Help You Win

The Pro-T Formation is one of football's most potent passing formations. The three pass receivers on the line of scrimmage and the two setbacks' alignments are in five positions for running pass patterns or blocking for the passer. This formation lends itself to straight drop-back passes, although the Triple Option sequences have added a new twist to play-action passes.

The Pro Sweep is a featured running play from this formation. Both the inside Triple Option and the Outside Veer series have helped to make the Pro-T Formation a more modernized and balanced run-pass formation.

Naturally, a strong-armed quarterback is a pre-requisite for selecting this formation as your basic offensive attack. The passer must have a quick release and the strong-arm ability to complete the sideline and the deep post and flag patterns.

## Advantages of the Pro-T Formation

1. The two wide-outs, the split end, and the flanker force the defense to defend against this attack in both width and depth.

2. This formation lends itself to a wide-open passing attack.

3. The Triple Option to the split side and the Pro Sweep to the tight end's side give this formation a balanced sweeping attack.

4. The stop-the-clock and catch-up attacks are easily executed from this wide-open formation.

5. The trap and the quick-hitters help to keep the interior defenders honest versus the straight ahead running attack.

6. Three quick receivers on or near the line of scrimmage and two setbacks give this formation a potent drop-back passing attack.

7. The alignment of the two wide-outs allows these two potential receivers to maneuver versus a normal "one-on-one-like" defensive pass coverage.

8. The alignment of the setbacks sets up a balanced, drop-back pocket pass protection unit.

9. The tight end's alignment gives this formation a strong short yardage and goal line attack to the tight side.

10. The draws, screens, and shuffle passes are natural long gainers using this wide offensive attack.

## Requirements of the Pro-T Personnel

*Quarterback*—He must be selected primarily for his passing potential. The quarterback must be an adequate runner, keeping the ball off the Triple Option series. He must have a strong passing arm to be able to throw the sideline and flag pass patterns to the two offensive wide-outs.

*Running Backs*—Just as their name implies, the setbacks must be good running backs. These two backs must also be solid pass blockers to give the passer sound protection when using the straight drop-back pocket passes, and they must be able to make the pro block and the lead block off the Triple Option series. The running backs must also have the ability to catch the quick release passes off the drop-back pass plays.

*Tight End*—This player must be a big, strong, durable blocker and pass receiver. He should have the blocking potential of an offensive tackle and should have the ability to make the key catch when the wide receivers are double teamed. This blocker must be able to make the one-on-one block on the goal line or execute the double team block on short yardage power plays.

*Tackles*—These blockers must anchor the Pro-T Formation.

They must be big enough and quick enough to block their assigned defender on all drop-back pass plays. These two linemen must be able to make the drive and power blocks so the running attack can go against all defensive fronts.

*Guards*—The guards must have pulling ability to lead the Pro Sweep and make the key trap block at the point of the attack. The guards must also be able to handle the defender on a one-on-one fire-out block and to adequately protect the drop-back passer.

*Center*—Must be the quickest man off the ball. He must be able to make the cut-off block and to reach block the frontside defender. He must be a good pass blocker and have the ability to pick up the free defender when the pivot is uncovered.

## The Pro Formation Alignment

The two running backs line up approximately four and one-half yards deep, splitting the inside leg of the offensive tackle with their bodies' midline. The tight end lines up one to three yards away from the strong-side offensive tackle. His split depends on the play called previously in the huddle. The wide-outs' (flanker and split end) splits are dependent upon field position and the play to be run (Diagram 2-1).

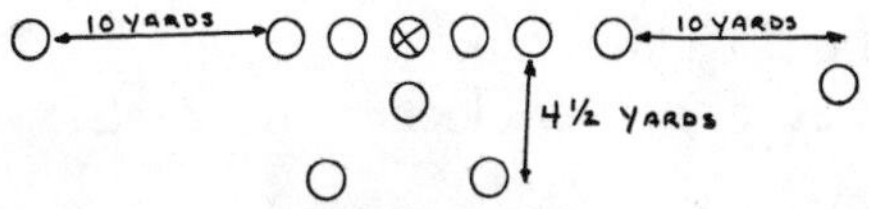

**Diagram 2-1**

## Attacking the Defensive Corner With the Pro Sweep

The best way to attack the defensive corner is to use a two-way weapon that threatens the opposition's outside flank and their off tackle hole on the same offensive maneuver. The Pro Sweep is one of the most successful methods of attacking the defensive perimeter.

Actually, the Pro Sweep develops into an off tackle play if the defensive end attempts to take away the wide threat of our running attack.

The ball carrier is instructed to run for daylight. He has the option of cutting off tackle behind our sealing guard's block or turning the corner wide if we can finesse block the defensive end to the inside.

The Pro Sweep is based upon the option blocking by our linemen combined with the option running of our ball carrier. Therefore, there is no one set or predetermined hole that the ball carrier must run through. Rather, we teach our blockers to block the defenders any way they want to go, and we tell the ball carrier to select any hole he may want to hit along the line of scrimmage. This current method of option blocking and running has become popular with the advent of the stemming and blitzing techniques of today's defenses.

The popularity of the Pro Sweep has an added attraction for all offensive strategists because this sweep can be run off of many favorite, wide-open, pass-oriented offensive formations. Not only can this sweep be run off the many spread "pro-type" formations, but it can also be launched off the Slot Formation. When we run the Pro Sweep off our slot formation, we do not have to change any of our blocking assignments or techniques. The ball carrier still executes his cut-for-daylight technique off our split end's shadow block.

The Pro Sweep can also be run toward or away from the flanker back. Diagram 2-2 points out the adaptation of the sweep off the Slot Formation. The advantages of running the sweep toward the slot are:

1.  Presents a new position and angle for our halfback to block the first man outside of our tackle's block.

2.  Gives the offense another blocker (the frontside running back) against the defense.

3.  Gives the offense another formation from which to run our pro sweep.

4.  Attacks the corner off a relatively tight formation.

5.  Provides a potential wide play off a primary power running offensive formation.

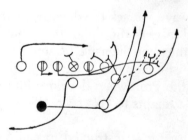

**Diagram 2-2**

6. Gives the Slot Formation a strong outside threat away from the slot man, without using motion.

The Pro Sweep is not based on speed, but rather on the more intelligent ball carrier who can help set up his blockers with advantageous angles as well as break for any opening off the blocker's option blocks. To allow the ball carrier time and space to carry out his option running, the offensive linemen must seal off the defensive penetration.

In developing this explosive sweeping weapon, we feel there are four important coaching points that must be perfected to successfully threaten the opposition's outside perimeter. These coaching points are:

1. *The route of the running back must emphasize the inside-out or the outside-in running route to successfully set up our pulling guard's and "shadow" end's blocking angles (Diagram 2-2).* If the runner successfully sets up his blockers, he will easily make them look good. The blockers, in turn, will make the ball carrier look good by consistently springing him into the open for long break-away runs.

The ball carrier's inside-out and outside-in routes are practiced each day in individual, group, and team drills. In the team drills, it is advantageous to have two running backs run the pulling guards' routes while their fellow players are in the running back sets, so the "guards" can experience for themselves the problems encountered by our pulling guards. As soon as the offense goes into team drills, the ball carriers have a more instinctive knowledge of how to run the correct route from the offensive guards' pulling assignments.

The running backs also take their turns as offensive ends and go through the correct procedures of the "shadow" block from a two yard "nasty" split position. We use the term "nasty" because this two yard split is the most difficult split for a defender to play. The end is not actually a split end; nor is he a tight end; he is just in a "nasty" inbetween split.

It has been our experience that if all players understand each other's assignments, it will make each player react and play more intelligently regarding his own specific assignments.

The running backs are also taught that they have the ability to use option running. Option running means that the ball carrier can level off for the goal line or cut upfield anytime he sees daylight. He also has the option to take an inside-out angle and head for the flag whenever the defense stacks up the inside game. Option running affords the intelligent runner a chance to use his own native ability by setting up our linemen's option blocking.

2. *The pulling guards are the touchdown makers on this particular power sweep.* Both of these pulling linemen must run like clockwork along with the ball carrier in order to successfully break away for the big play. Our backside guard's assignment is to seal off the backside defensive pursuit by turning up quickly into the off tackle hole and to seal block to the inside. As the sealing guard turns up to the inside, he must pick up any pursuing defender. He has the option to (a) block his inside gap, (b) turn upfield inside of his offensive end, or (c) turn upfield outside of the "shadow" blocking offensive end. Therefore, our backside guard has option blocking just as our running back has option running. The backside guard's option running technique is predicated upon the defensive play and pursuit of the opposition's defense (Diagram 2-3).

The frontside guard's assignment is to pull to his frontside with depth, clearing our offensive back's block, and kick out the first opponent outside of our offensive end's block. This is usually the defensive contain man—the end on a six or eight man line, or the cornerback on a four or five man alignment (Diagram 2-4).

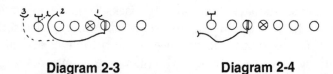

| Diagram 2-3 | Diagram 2-4 |

3. *The frontside or playside end's "shadow" block is the key that the ball carrier looks for as he takes his third step back after receiving the football.* The offensive end's strategy in taking the two yard split is to isolate the defensive end. The "shadow" block is executed by the end taking a two yard or "nasty" split from his tackle. When the ball is snapped, the offensive end drops his inside foot back first to protect the all-important inside gap. If the defender fires to the inside, the end blocks him in by keeping his head in front of the defender, driving him down the line of scrimmage. He must prevent more than a one and one-half yard penetration (Diagram 2-5a).

If the defensive end flows to the outside, the offensive end shadow blocks him by turning him to the outside, blocking him high, and screening the defender the way he wants to go (Diagram 2-5b). The term "shadow" is used to describe how the offensive end follows the defensive end's every move.

If the defender plays nose-up on our frontside offensive end and does not commit himself, we teach our blocker to set up for two counts, "shadow" the defender, then go after him with a hard-nosed shoulder block (Diagram 2-5c).

If the defensive end attempts to crash directly over the offensive end, the blocker must block the ramming defender as aggressively as the defender attacks him (Diagram 2-5d).

**Diagram 2-5a**

**Diagram 2-5b**

**Diagram 2-5c**

**Diagram 2-5d**

On all of the offensive end's "shadow" blocks, he must be taught to scramble after the defender until the final whistle blows as the ball carrier cuts off his block. Therefore, the offensive end never knows where the running back will make his final cut.

4. *The playside (frontside) back is taught to use a unique block which we refer to as the "chopper" block.* The technique used in this block is to aim at the patella or knee cap of the first defender on or outside of the offensive tackle. The frontside back aims his inside shoulder at his target and sprints directly toward, and drives his shoulder forcefully into, the defender's knee.

The defender is usually drawn inside by the offensive tackle's inside route, thus setting up a perfect angle for our blocking back. Regardless of the size of the defender or the offensive back, this blocking technique has proved to be successful in the high school, college, and professional ranks. The blocker's entire body protects the defender's pursuit path, regardless of whether he knocks down the defender or not. The "chopper" block is never practiced live man-on-man—only on a large stand-up dummy. Once the smaller blocker has mastered the shoulder chop technique, he will enjoy knocking down the larger defensive linemen. The blocker is taught to bend the upper portion of his body forward when approaching his target, and to fully extend his body with a powerful shoulder thrust when smashing into his target. This is the same technique that the professional backs employ in cutting down the giant front four linemen of the defensive professional ranks.

## Blocking the Oklahoma Defense

Blocking the conventional Oklahoma Defense presents no problem as shown in Diagram 2-6. Against the Oklahoma Defense, the blocking rules are:

*Frontside End*—Split two yards; block any man covering you, block inside, or block the linebacker. Sustain your block, as timing is the important ingredient in this play.

*Frontside Tackle*—Split one yard and always be ready to block your inside gap (stepping with your inside foot); if no one is there, block the linebacker or any man who comes into that area.

*Frontside Guard*—Pull, gaining depth, and clear the end's block; kick out on the first enemy outside of the end's block. If the end turns his opponent to the outside, turn up to the inside and be ready to seal. Lose about three yards in depth prior to turning upfield.

*Center*—Block man over; if no one is there, block to the frontside (playside).

*Backside Guard*—Block your inside gap; if no one is there, pull and block the first enemy who shows. You can pull inside or outside of your offensive end's block. Read the offensive end's block.

*Backside Tackle*—Pull and fill the pulling guard's area; if no one shows, continue past the guard's area, turn upfield through the first daylight area, and seal.

*Backside End*—Sprint crossfield shallow and throw a block on the first enemy who shows.

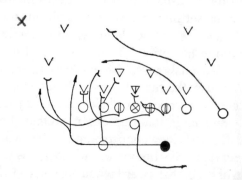

**Diagram 2-6**

*Flanker Back (To Frontside)*—Drive off the line of scrimmage for five yards, then crack-back block on the second deep man. *(To Backside)*—Run a short post route and block the middle area.

*Frontside Back (Blocker)*—Take a lead step with your outside foot to get an outside-in angle on the defender. Aim at the defensive man's patella (knee cap) and unload on him, using your inside shoulder to chop down the defender.

*Quarterback*—Pivot on your backside foot one hundred and eighty degrees (half turn) and hand off to the backside back. Continue in the opposite direction of the ball carrier on a bootleg course.

*Ball Carrier*—Take a lead step with your frontside foot. The second step is a cross-over step; on the third step, the ball carrier should begin to give ground. Keep your eye on the frontside end's "shadow" block and make your cut according to the action of our frontside end's block.

Using these blocking rules, there should be few problems blocking the straight Oklahoma Defense; however, more problems can occur when there are team and individual games off this defense. Therefore, we have diagrammed a couple of Oklahoma team stunts and how the blockers would pick up these games using the Pro Sweep's blocking assignments.

## Blocking the Oklahoma Pincher Stunt

If the defense uses a pincher stunt to the play side (the defensive tackle and end crash to the inside and the near linebacker scallops to the defensive end's original position), we would pick up this deal in the following manner (Diagram 2-7):

*Frontside Tackle*—Pick up the defensive tackle who immediately crosses your face and is shooting to the inside.

*Frontside Back*—Block the first man who shows outside of the tackle, the pinching defensive end.

*Frontside End*—Drive off to the inside for the defensive end who pinches inside; if you cannot pick up this angling defender, continue to the inside, changing your angle slightly, and pick up the scalloping linebacker. If the nearside linebacker has scalloped around you, he will be picked up by the pulling guard.

The ball carrier will break for daylight, usually just off the tail of the offensive end as the nearside linebacker scallops to the outside and is blocked in that same direction.

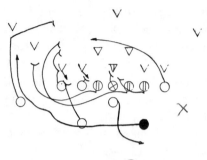

**Diagram 2-7**

## Blocking the Oklahoma Crash Stunt

When the defense employs the crash game (the defensive tackle pinches to the outside shoulder of our offensive guard's original position, and the linebacker crashes to fill for the vacated defensive tackle over the outside shoulder of our offensive tackle's original position), we pick up this stunt in the following manner (Diagram 2-8):

*Frontside Tackle*—Pick up the defensive tackle who quickly crosses in front of your face, angling to the inside.

*Frontside Back*—Block the first man who shows outside of the tackle, the crashing linebacker on this deal.

All of the other offensive football players' assignments would be similar to the regular offensive blocking techniques.

Daily football practice time must be spent blocking and reviewing the many Oklahoma defensive games. Walk through it, run it half speed, and then scrimmage it full speed. After a few weeks, the player's rules and variations according to the team stunts become second nature to all offensive players.

Practice time must also be used blocking the many defensive looks or defenses. While each defense will have its own variations, we will review only the straight defenses in this group.

In attacking the Wide Tackle Six or 60 Defense, you may end up with a double team on the defensive guard to the front or play side (Diagram 2-9). The frontside back chops down the linebacker as he is the first man on or outside the offensive tackle. The linebacker is often a more difficult defender to cut down as he is in a more balanced stance and is often a more agile defender than a lineman in a four-point stance. Therefore, the frontside back must be more aggressive and take a good outside-in angle on this defender. The blocker must

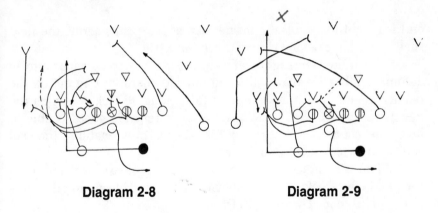

**Diagram 2-8**                    **Diagram 2-9**

also raise his hips as he chops at the linebacker's knee cap so that the defender cannot step over the blocker.

The frontside end may have to readjust his two yard split if the defensive tackle lines up in the end's inside gap. Now, the end can only take a one yard split and must block down on the inside man, keeping his head in front of the defender and cutting off his penetration. The frontside guard must be ready to block the end quickly as he pulls, because his man will now be on the line of scrimmage and therefore will be closer to the pulling guard's position.

The flanker again blocks the second deep man, who now becomes the middle safetyman in the three deep secondary. The backside end aims across the field with his sights on the farside defensive halfback.

All of the other offensive assignments are similar to our power sweep against the Oklahoma front.

When we attack the Gap or Goal Line Defense, we use the following special coaching points for our frontside end and our frontside back:

*Coaching Point (Frontside End):* When the defensive end is in your defensive gap and pinches or moves away from you, adjust your course and pick up the nearest inside linebacker.

*Coaching Point (Frontside Back):* Block the defensive end who is in the gap between the offensive end and tackle. Be ready for the defender to pinch to the inside.

Therefore, against a gap eight defense, our frontside tackle and end block down to the inside, and our frontside guard pulls and kicks out the end man on the line of scrimmage. The frontside back cuts down the next defender to the inside; the center cuts off the defensive guard, as does our backside guard and backside tackle. The backside end is taught to cut off the inside man as he sprints across the field shallow on his blocking course (Diagram 2-10).

Against the Gap Eight Defense, the Pro Sweep develops into an automatic off tackle play with our frontside guard kicking out on the defensive end. The only exception to running off tackle is when the defensive end pinches so tightly that our frontside guard is able to hook the contain man and cut him down, thus enabling the ball carrier to swing wide around the corner.

When we run against the Six-One (6-1) Defense, we zero in on the middle linebacker. Both our center and frontside guard take shots at the point man (Diagram 2-11).

*Frontside End*—Shadow block the man over.

*Frontside Tackle*—Block down on the defensive guard.

*Frontside Guard*—Pull, turn upfield inside of the offensive end, and seal block the scalloping middle linebacker.

*Center*—Block the man over (middle linebacker) by taking the correct frontside angle. Block the middle linebacker where he will be rather than where he is lined up.

*Backside Guard*—Pull, turn upfield into a space of daylight, and look for the middle linebacker. If he does not show first, you should pick up any pursuing defender.

*Frontside Back*—Chop down the defensive tackle using your prescribed chop block.

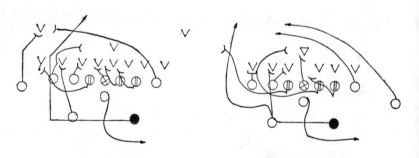

**Diagram 2-10**          **Diagram 2-11**

This is somewhat of a professional defense with the middle linebacker. If this point man can be eliminated, the chances for a successful play are greatly enhanced.

When facing a gap stack defense such as a Right Stack Oklahoma Defense, the offensive linemen must block the stack "look." In this defense, the offensive blockers must recognize the chance of a deal by the stack men, a gap fire charge by the near stack man, or the possibility of a stack key defense when all deep stacked defenders are hedging on a particular offensive target (Diagram 2-12).

## Blocking the Gap Stack

The quarterback should be instructed to call the stack; the frontside end should recognize the stack, as well as the three defenders to his inside, and be ready to block the scalloping linebacker.

*Frontside End*—Block the linebacker or any pursuing defender.

*Frontside Tackle*—Block the man to your inside (since our center is cutting off the gapped middle guard, he is told to pick up the frontside or backside linebacker).

*Frontside Guard*—Pull and block the contain man the way he is playing—shuffling to the outside.

*Center*—Cut off the man to your frontside gap.

*Backside Guard*—Pull and seal block along with the frontside end.

*Frontside Back*—Chop down the tackle using the chopping block technique.

## Blocking the Eagle Defense

When blocking the Eagle Defense (Diagram 2-13), we end up with a double team block on the frontside or playside Eagle linebacker. The frontside end blocks to his inside and the frontside back fires straight into the Eagle linebacker.

*Frontside End*—Block down on the Eagle linebacker.

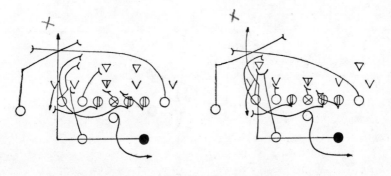

Diagram 2-12               Diagram 2-13

*Frontside Tackle*—Drive down on the defensive tackle, stepping down with your inside foot and keeping your head in front of the defender.

*Frontside Guard*—Pull and block outside on the contain man.

*Center*—Block man over, keeping your head between the defensive middle guard and the ball carrier.

*Backside Guard*—Pull, losing ground, then turn upfield at the first opening. Seal to the inside.

*Frontside Back*—Block the Eagle linebacker along with the frontside end. The blocking back becomes the post man and the end becomes the drive man. The immediate pressure from the frontside end helps to set up the defensive linebacker for the frontside back's block.

## How to Block the 7-1 Defense

Running against the Seven Diamond (7-1) Defense again presents the problem of blocking the middle linebacker or point man in this defense. With a seven man defensive line in front of the middle linebacker, it becomes a most difficult task to block this defender on many power sweeps. Utilizing the Pro Sweep, our offensive blockers are able to see the point man by sealing this defender with our offensive tackle as well as the pulling backside guard (Diagram 2-14).

*Frontside End*—Shadow block the defensive man who plays over any part of you.

*Frontside Tackle*—Block to the inside, being careful that the middle linebacker does not blitz into the gap vacated by our pulling frontside guard. Be ready for the defensive linebacker attempting to scallop out and around you.

*Frontside Guard*—Pull deep enough to clear the frontside back's

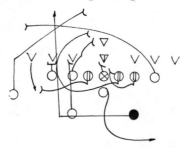

**Diagram 2-14**

block and kick out the first defender outside of our end's block. This defender should be outside conscious; therefore, you should have an easy angle for the kick-out block.

*Center*—Cut-off block the middle guard positioned over you. Take a quick step with your frontside foot and block the "Mike" man where he will be rather than where he lines up.

*Backside Guard*—Pull and be ready to turn upfield at the first opening. This should be just inside of the offensive end's shadow block. Seal block anyone who shows to the inside. Watch for the scalloping linebacker.

*Backside Tackle*—Cut off the inside seam. Pull right behind the pulling backside guard, filling all the way over to the center-guard gap in case of a middle blitz. If no one shows, continue behind the backside pulling guard's route, filling in wherever necessary.

*Frontside Back*—Chop block the defender over or just outside of the offensive tackle. The defender should step to the inside if he is keying the offensive tackle, making the chop block an easier assignment.

## Blocking the Split-Six Defense

Recently, one of the more popular defenses has become the Split-Six Defense. This eight man front has caused several blocking problems for the offensive strategists because of the flowing linebackers and the gap look. The blocking assignments of the Pro Sweep offer no blocking problems against this defense, as most of the offensive players have fine blocking angles as diagrammed and described below (Diagram 2-15).

*Frontside End*—Block the defensive end to the outside, as the defender has outside contain responsibility.

*Frontside Tackle*—Block down on the defensive guard in the guard-center gap. You must step with your frontside foot and keep your head in front of the defender, blocking him to the inside with your backside shoulder.

*Frontside Guard*—Pull and turn up inside of the end's block, or swing around outside of the end's "shadow" block. Your route depends on the defensive play of the contain man coupled with the block of the frontside end.

*Center*—Step with your frontside foot and cut off the defensive linebacker. You must move fast on this cut-off block, as the defender is a linebacker and is already in the gap.

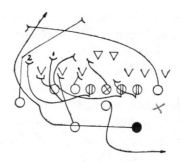

**Diagram 2-15**

*Backside Guard*—Pull and turn up in first opening.

*Backside Tackle*—Pull and seal to the inside wherever necessary. Your pulling technique must be under control similar to a scalloping linebacker. Against the Split-Six Defense, you may have to fill to the inside center-guard gap, as the backside or offside linebacker may try to shoot into the vacated backside guard's original position.

*Frontside Back*—Cut down the defensive tackle with a chop block.

One of the most advantageous reasons for using the Pro Sweep is that it may be run from a multiple-formation offense. We can run the Pro Sweep from the full house, using the fullback as a fullback power threat (Diagram 2-16). The quarterback can also give him an empty-hand fake before his customary pro hand-off.

The Slot Formation Run utilizes the slotback to block the first man on or outside of our offensive tackle. The slot man may often have a better angle for blocking than in his regular set backfield position (Diagram 2-17).

With the Split Slot Formation, we can use the frontside setback as a lead blocker for our pro sweep. The lead blocker can be most effective in picking up a defensive leakage and for that extra block at the point of attack. We have used this extra blocker to keep the

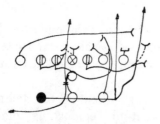

**Diagram 2-16**

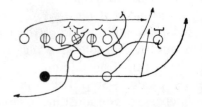

**Diagram 2-17**

outside defender who is aligned over our offensive frontside end, honest, by not only fighting our end's block but also by getting rid of our set back's inside-out blocking angle.

In using the Slot Formation, we can also use a flanker away from the slot and run the Pro Sweep to either side, depending on which side we choose to place our running back.

## Blocking Technique Checklist

### Frontside End:

*Purpose*: Shadow block the defender, taking him any way he wants to flow.

*Stance*: Two-point or three-point, depending on your split; use a parallel stance so you can block in any direction.

*Split*: Two yards to isolate the defensive end; protect inside gap first; adjust split, depending on the defensive end's position.

*Approach*: Don't fire out on the snap; be ready to cut off the defender if he shoots inside gap; set up low and wait for the defender to make the first move.

*Contact*: Block high with a shadow block; fire high, not out; block as tough as the defender is; don't give ground; block the defender the way he wants to go.

*Blocks*: Four techniques that may be used by the shadow blocking end include:

1. Defender penetrates: Stop penetration by stepping to the inside with your frontside foot; keep your head in front of the defender to cut off penetration; drive him down the line.

2. Defender flows to outside: Turn outside on the defender; screen him outside, blocking high; run him outside the way he wants to go.

3. Defender crashes straight into you: Stop penetration by firing into him; fight pressure, block as tough as he is; don't allow him to penetrate more than one yard.

4. Defender plays waiting game and will not commit himself: Take two counts and go after him; put your nose into him and drive him off the line of scrimmage; take him the way he fights your block.

*Follow-Through*: Scramble after the defender until the whistle blows; the ball carrier will be late and must cut off your block; if you lose your balance, scramble after the defender on all fours; timing is more important than speed on this play.

## Backside End:

*Purpose*: Block downfield to help the ball carrier break away for a score.

*Stance*: Regular three-point if tight, or two-point if split.

*Approach*: Cut off the inside defender; take a shallow course crossfield and throw a block on the first odd-colored jersey.

*Contact*: Get as close to the defender as possible (step on his toes) and use a cross-body block; roll your hips on contact and throw through the defender.

## Frontside Tackle:

*Purpose*: Step with your inside foot to protect the guard's area; if no one is there, continue through and take the linebacker.

*Stance*: Regular.

*Approach:* Short jab step with the inside foot; your second step should be longer, but short enough to maintain balance; if no man is in the guard's area, readjust your course and take the linebacker; fire at where the man will be rather than where he is.

*Contact*: Keep your head in front of the defender to stop his penetration; drive through the opponent with your outside shoulder; run over the defender; use a shoulder block on the linebacker and don't let him scallop around you—cut off his pursuit.

*Follow-Through*: Keep your feet digging until the whistle blows; as a last resort only, go into a cross-body block.

## Backside Tackle:

*Purpose*: Pull and fill the backside guard's area if the man in the guard's area is free. If the center is blocking this area, turn through the first daylight opening and cut down anyone within three yards of the line of scrimmage.

*Stance*: Regular, but place more weight on your backside foot than on the hand.

*Approach*: Step first with a short jab step with your play-side foot; drive hard off your backside foot; take a longer second step, but keep it short enough to maintain balance; stay low and under control; be ready to turn upfield to fill into any open area.

*Contact*: Fill block or block any man within three yards of the line of scrimmage; the type of block to use depends on position of defender—usually use a cut-off block, maintaining balance by staying on all fours.

*Follow-Through*: Scramble on all fours, keeping your butt ahead of the ball carrier until the whistle blows.

### Frontside Guard:

*Purpose*: Pull out, losing depth, to block the first defender outside of the frontside end's block; upon reaching the end's block, you can go inside or outside of it.

*Stance*: Regular, placing more weight on your backside foot than on the hand.

*Approach*: Your first step should be a short jab with the playside foot; snap your arm back to the side to which you're pulling; drive hard off your backside foot; take a longer second step, but keep it short enough to maintain balance; keep low with elbows close to the body to maintain balance; sprint under control at top speed; the course depends on defender; clear the halfback's block, gaining depth (belly back); sprint past the offensive end's block and adjust your angle according to the defender's charge; never pass up one man to get to another.

*Contact*: The block depends on the location and position of the defender; the ball carrier will set up your block; since you have a fine angle and room to maneuver, use a crossfield block; step on the defender's toes so you won't be "throwing" your body at him; run a shoulder right through the defensive man.

*Follow-Through*: Roll hips on contact; roll three times after blocking.

### Backside Guard:

*Purpose*: Pull out laterally down the line of scrimmage and seal to the inside at first opening.

*Stance*: Regular, placing more weight on your backside foot than on the hand.

*Approach*: Jab step with your frontside foot; drive hard off the backside foot; snap your arm back to the side to which you're pulling; the second step will be longer, but short enough to maintain balance; sprint under control; stay close to the line of scrimmage; turn upfield, tight off the frontside halfback's block; dip your inside shoulder as you turn upfield; be ready to meet a defender in the hole; never pass up one defender for another; use short, choppy, controlled steps as you turn upfield for the seal block; go after the defender—don't wait for him.

*Contact*: The block depends on the location and position of defender; use a running shoulder block when sealing; if this block isn't possible, use a crossfield technique.

*Follow-Through*: Run through your opponent or roll three times, depending on which block you select.

### Frontside Back:

*Purpose*: Chop down the first man on the outside of the offensive tackle.

*Stance*: Regular three-point.

*Approach*: Take a proper angle to cut off the defender's pursuit; take a short jab step with your frontside foot; push off with the backside foot; take a proper course so you can block the defender with your inside shoulder.

*Contact*: Knock down the defender with a kneecap chop block; use your inside shoulder on contact; extend your body, keeping your head to the opponent's outside; drive through the defender; keep your butt high to cut off pursuit or a jumping opponent.

*Follow Through*: Keep driving your legs forward on contact; continue to roll until the whistle.

### Running Back:

*Purpose*: Read the frontside end's block and make your cut off it.

*Stance*: Regular three-point.

*Approach*: Take a short lead step with your frontside foot to receive the ball from the quarterback; cross over on your second step; give ground on the third step to help set up the timing for your blockers; read the frontside end's "shadow" block; make your cut according to daylight; if you're going wide, make an inside-out cut and head for the flag; if you're going inside, make an outside-in cut and level off, dip your shoulder, put your head down, and run like a fullback.

*Follow Through*: Always make that second effort; keep your legs driving until the whistle.

### Flanker Back:

*Purpose*: Block downfield to help the ball carrier break away.

*Stance*: Regular two-point.

*Approach*: If flanked to frontside, drive off the line for five yards, then crack back on the second deep defender; if flanked to backside, run a short post pattern and block down the middle.

*Contact*: Step on the defender's toes and use a cross-body block; block through the defender by rolling your hips into the block.

*Follow Through*: Roll three times.

**Quarterback (Ball Handling Techniques):**

*Purpose*: Get the ball to the ball carrier and bootleg fake in the opposite direction.

*Stance*: Regular T-Formation.

*Approach*: Use your left foot as the pivot foot; make a half turn with your backside foot and go straight back to hand off to the ball carrier. Hand off to the backside back and continue your bootleg course.

*Follow Through*: Don't watch the ball carrier; continue your bootleg course away from the ball carrier's route.

Another method of getting outside is the Outside Triple Option Veer play.

## The Complete Outside Triple Option Veer Play

The quarterback rides the frontside running back a hole wider and gives the ball to the dive back if the #3 defender steps across the line of scrimmage or shuffles to the outside. Since both the frontside offensive tackle and end are two-timing the #2 defender, the hole is there. If the #3 defender closes down and attacks the dive back (Diagram 2-18), the quarterback is instructed to keep the ball and check the #4 defender. If the #4 man attacks the quarterback, he

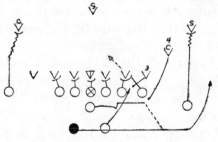

**Diagram 2-18**

pitches the ball to the trailing back. Naturally, if the #4 defender feathers to his outside or attempts to attack the pitchman, the quarterback is coached to cut upfield and run his keeper play. The flanker executes his run-off block on the widest secondary defender.

The reason for the great success of the Outside Veer Dive play is that the #3 defender is normally assigned to tackle the quarterback on the normal Triple Option maneuver. If the #3 defender executes correctly and the offense runs the Outside Veer play, the Veer Dive play is a natural long gainer (Diagram 2-19).

If the #3 defender tackles the dive back and the #4 defender contains the pitchman all the way, the quarterback is left all alone to run the quarterback keeper play (Diagram 2-20).

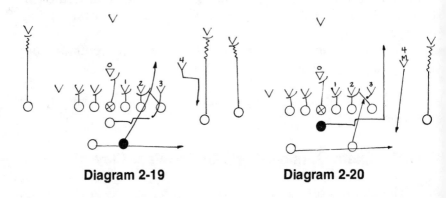

Diagram 2-19                                   Diagram 2-20

## The Triple "G" Outside Veer Attack

The Triple "G" Outside Veer offense features the frontside guard pulling and leading the second (quarterback keeper) and the third (pitch-out to the trailing back) phases of the Triple Option play. When attacking to the flanker side of the offense, we like to double team the defensive tackle versus the Oklahoma 52 Defense. The quarterback checks the #3 defender and pulls the ball out of the dive back's pocket whenever the #3 man attacks the dive back (Diagram 2-21). The key blocker is the frontside pulling guard. He is coached to pull deep enough to clear the double team block by the frontside tackle and end, and block the #3 defender with his inside shoulder if the #3 defender is attacking the quarterback. If the defensive #3 man hangs, the pulling guard is coached to pull in front of this defender and block him back with an outside-in angle if the #3 defender does not attack the dive back (Diagram 2-22).

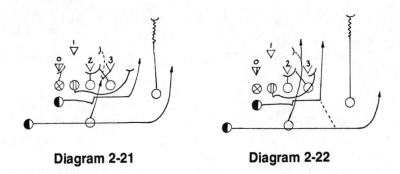

Diagram 2-21          Diagram 2-22

The key coaching point is that the quarterback is able to ride the diveback a little longer because of the inside shoulder block of the frontside pulling guard. The pulling guard must be ready to block the defensive #3 man right away with the inside shoulder. The flanker back must be well schooled in the different defensive perimeter schemes of the deep secondary defenders. The quarterback must hug the line of scrimmage and not stray off the line, because of the pulling technique of the offensive guard. This would also ruin the four-by-four-yard potential ratio between the quarterback and the pitchman. The driving tight end must be ready to use the co-op block and pick up the scalloping 52 inside linebacker if the offensive post man (tackle) can block the defensive tackle (#2) by himself (Diagram 2-23).

The Outside Veer (with the pulling frontside guard) helps to set up the quarterback's Triple Option Veer passing series. This pass series is of great success because the quarterback always has the option of passing or running the ball. The defense gives him the key to pass or run. This key comes off the quarterback's read, on the move, of the defensive secondary's scheme of attack. Naturally, if the quarterback is fortunate enough to face a status quo secondary, which never changes its perimeter and secondary attack, he may know his option prior to the snap of the ball. But in today's multi-defensive secondary stunts in both high school and college football, the signal

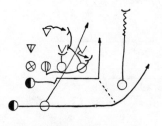

Diagram 2-23

caller must be well aware of the many secondary stunts he may face prior to facing each opponent.

The flanker must read three different coverages by the outside four deep cornerback:

*First*: The cornerback levels off and plays the flat in a two deep pass coverage. Normally, the cornerback will attempt to chug the flanker and force the receiver to the inside. The flanker is coached to run his streak pattern, forcing the deep safety to his side as deep as possible; then the wide receiver runs a comeback pattern between the cornerback's and safetyman's zones. The flanker's comeback pattern is predicated upon the timing of when the passer gets to his set-up area versus the two-deep, five-underneath zone (Diagram 2-24).

*Second*: The cornerback plays a Monster-like position and levels off into the flat as the deep outside defender covers his deep outside one-third zone. The flanker is coached to fight his way outside of the leveling defender, then run his comeback curl pattern in, between the leveling outside short flat zone and the deep outside one-third zone (Diagram 2-25).

*Third*: If the cornerback begins to turn and run deep with the flanker back, the wide receiver continues to run off the cornerback, plants his outside foot, and hooks back for a well-timed hook pass. This is true when the cornerback takes his deep outside zone on a safety force or man-to-man pass defense (Diagram 2-26).

## Triple Option to Monster

Many offensive coaches like to run the Triple Option play away from the Monster defender. When this philosophy is adopted, the

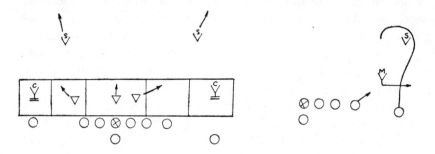

Diagram 2-24                 Diagram 2-25

offense finds itself running continually into the sidelines or to the short side of the field. In order to make the Triple Option play go to the wide side or the Monster's side, a man-on-man blocking call should be emphasized, and the Triple Option play should look like Diagram 2-27. Man blocking techniques for the playside offensive guard and tackle will be explained later in the chapter.

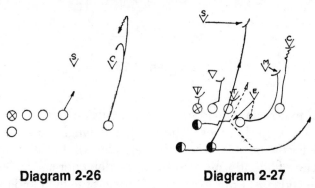

Diagram 2-26                    Diagram 2-27

## Tight End's Triple Option Junction Block

The basic objective of all Triple Option attacks is to get the pitch off and turn the corner. This means use the third dimension of the Triple Option and run wide around the opposition's flank. This is a sound offensive objective, but there are times when the offense is on a hash mark and strategy dicatates a Triple Option maneuver to the short side of the field. There are also times when the opponent's defensive contain man takes away the wide sweep by containing the third phase of the Triple Option (pitch-out) with a secondary defender, linebacker, or defensive end. Therefore, in order to get the pitch off to the primary sweeping threat, the offensive strategy dictates creating a running lane *inside* of the defensive containment. This means the offensive blocker would be required to kick out (we call it a "Junction" block) the containing defender. Thus, the offense creates a running lane that forces the defensive pursuit to attack the pitchman upfield rather than in a lateral pursuit course.

Diagram 2-28 points out the Junction block by the tight end, who blocks the containing cornerback to the outside. The tight end steps upfield two steps and anticipates a containing path by the defender. The offensive anticipation is caused by the alignment of the cornerback to the strong side of the offensive formation. The tight end is

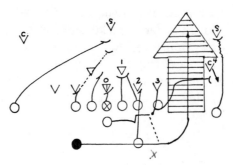

**Diagram 2-28**

coached to take an upfield step with his outside foot and then push off
the second step (left foot). The blocker is taught to strike a course
directly for the position where the defender will be rather than where
he is. The tight end runs directly at the defender and slides his head
to the outside just prior to contact. We want the tight end to block the
containing defender with his inside shoulder so the defender cannot
pursue the ball carrier upfield. This means that if the blocker is to lose
the contain man, he must block only to his (the blocker's) inside,
which will force the defender out of position to make the tackle. The
flanker is coached to use his run-off block on the widest secondary
defender.

　　If the defensive #3 man attacks the quarterback, the ball handler
pitches back to the trailing running back, and the ball carrier cuts up
inside of the tight end's Junction block. The ball carrier runs for
daylight into the "arrowed area" in Diagram 2-28.

　　If the defensive secondary lines up in a four-across-the-board
alignment and attempts to revolve based upon the flow of the ball, the
tight end again uses a Junction block. This time the tight end Junction
blocks the outside secondary defender who is assigned to roll up and
contain the pitch-out threat. Since the offense still wants to get the
ball to the gamebreaker (left halfback), the tight end kicks the corner
back to the outside while the flankerback uses his run-off block on the
inside strong safetyman, who is revolving to cover the deep outside
one-third zone (Diagram 2-29). Since the pitchback is forced to cut
the sweep up closer to the inside than in the normal wide sweep, it is
imperative that the interior offensive linemen seal off the inside pursuing defenders. This means the frontside offensive tackle is assigned
to execute a combo block on the #1 defender, with his main assignment to cut off the pursuit lane of the #0 linebacker (Diagram 2-29).

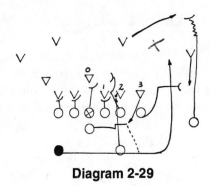

**Diagram 2-29**

## Man Blocking

Many times coaches will select man-on-man blocking when running the basic Triple Option. Coaches select this blocking adjustment to protect their fullbacks from being hit head-on by the first defender outside of the frontside (playside) offensive tackle's normal down or veer blocking assignment.

Against the Oklahoma (52) Defense, the basic blocking adjustment is illustrated in Diagram 2-30. The frontside guard steps toward the defensive tackle with his outside foot and checks the defensive tackle's route. If the defensive tackle does not slant down toward the guard, he then steps upfield and attempts to cut off the defensive inside linebacker. The frontside offensive tackle blocks the defensive #2 man on his normal man blocking assignment.

If the defensive tackle slants down, the offensive guard must step in his direction and pick him up immediately (Diagram 2-31). The offensive tackle sees the defensive tackle slant to the inside and steps directly upfield to cut off the linebacker's scrape technique as featured in Diagram 2-31.

Once the interior blockers have sealed off all of the defenders, the setback is coached to block the second defender outside of the

**Diagram 2-30**

**Diagram 2-31**

offensive tackle's block. The split end is coached to block the widest
deep defender.

*Coaching Point*: While this may not look like a true Triple Option
play because two defenders do not remain unblocked on or near the
line of scrimmage, it is a definite part of the Triple Option package.
This is one of the most dependable methods of attacking wide and
using the Monster defender as the target of the Triple Option attack.
The quarterback still has the three-part phase to exploit on this play.
He may give the ball to the fullback, keep the ball, or pitch the ball to
the pitchman. (Diagram 2-27 illustrates the three-segment part of the
attack.)

## The Sprint-Out Pass-Run Series

The Sprint-Out Pass-Run Series is usually run away from the
flanker to the split end's side of the offensive formation. This means
the frontside guard to the split end side uses his fire-out blocking
technique rather than pulling to lead the Sprint-Out series. The lead
back blocks the first defender outside of the offensive tackle's block.
The quarterback's primary receiver is the split end. He runs the same
pass patterns, depending on his outside deep defender's moves as
described previously by the flanker's three read-pass patterns. The
extra pass receiver is the pitchman, who continues past his pitch
course and turns upfield once the quarterback sets up for his pass.
The pitchman keeps looking for an option pitch until the passer sets
up. If the deep defensive back is run off and no defender takes the
flat, the quarterback drops a short pass off to the pitchman, who is
coached to cut upfield (Diagram 2-31a). If the quarterback is not forced
to pass by a safety, corner, or outside linebacker, the quarterback is
coached to carry out his option play and keep the ball on the option
keeper (Diagram 2-32).

In Diagram 2-32, the safetyman takes the flat while the outside

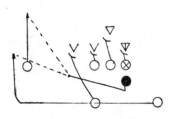

**Diagram 2-31a**

cornerback is run off by the split end. Thus, the quarterback has clear sailing to run his Sprint-Out keeper play. This means the quarterback may keep the ball, pitch out to the pitchman, pass to the split end, or pass to the pitchman turning upfield. A fifth phase of this Sprint-Out Pass-Run Series is the tight end running his shallow drag cut. He is often one of the most open receivers on all play-action pass series; if the passer can hit this dragging end, it will usually result in a long gainer (Diagram 2-33).

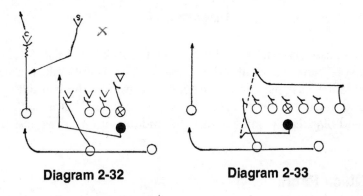

Diagram 2-32                         Diagram 2-33

The Sprint-Out Pass-Run Series can also be run to the tight end's side, with the tight end and the flankerback as two quick receivers to the sprint side.

## Counter Pass

The Counter Pass is an excellent pass to the split end side, because the counter backfield action slips the fullback free into the flat to the split end's side. This is particularly effective versus a man-to-man defense where the weak safety is responsible for the counter-ing halfback man-to-man. The outside defensive linebacker is as-signed to play the fullback man-to-man, but he may be entertained by the halfback's counter action, and just this split-second hesitation may allow the fullback to slip behind the defender and shake the receiver free into the flat. The fullback is coached to run the flat pattern five to ten yards deep into the flat. The specific depth of the fullback's cut depends on the coverage of the outside defensive linebacker.

Diagram 2-34 illustrates: (1) the linebacker falling off and picking up the fullback in the flat. Now the quarterback is taught to put the ball away and run. (2) If the linebacker rushes the rolling out quarter-

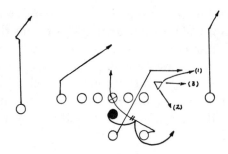

**Diagram 2-34**

back, the passer is coached to hit the free fullback in the flat. (3) If the linebacker "hangs" or waits, the fullback runs his optional, ten-yard deep sideline pass pattern and catches the ball on the run with the split end leading the escort. The tight end also helps with the downfield blocking, coming across the middle with his drag pass pattern.

## The Quick Pitch

The Quick Pitch to the split end side is a quick way to get around the corner to the weakside. This quick-pitch maneuver is also a fine play to incorporate into the Two Minute Stop-the Clock Attack, since it can be run into the sidelines to stop the clock.

The split tackle and the split guard quickly pull to lead the halfback's quick-pitch course. The split tackle pulls and takes a course to kick out the containing cornerback. The split guard is coached to pull and cut off the #3 defender's penetration. The split end is taught to crack back on the defensive #3 man, carrying out a post-like double team blocking assignment. Both the backside tackle and guard pull to cut off the opposition's possible seepage. The center blocks the middle guard one-on-one while the tight end blocks crossfield.

A quick pitch under the fullback's quick fake helps to spring the halfback loose on his lateral take-off course. The ball carrier is coached to key off the block of the tight end. If the offensive end kicks the containing cornerback out (Diagram 2-35), the ball carrier is taught to cut inside. If the tight end is able to overthrow on the cornerback and cut him down, the ball carrier is coached to turn the corner to the outside. The quarterback makes a reverse pivot and pitches the ball out to the halfback. Then he makes a quick fake to the fullback. The fullback fake helps to set up the fake-pitch give to the fullback in a play belonging to the quick-pitch sequence.

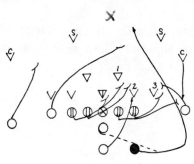

**Diagram 2-35**

## Quarterback's Defensive Secondary Looks

The quarterback must be able to read both the four deep and the three deep secondaries. Basically, these two reads are simple and are taught in the following progression:

*Three Deep Alignment:*

1. The two wide-out pass receivers' twenty-five to thirty yard spread normally isolates the middle safetyman (Diagram 2-36).
2. The width of the two wide receivers forces the two wide defensive backs into one-on-one coverage, regardless of the secondary zone or man-to-man defensive coverage call.
3. The underneath defenders usually play zone or may possibly be assigned man-to-man pass defense.
4. If the deep secondary is locked into a three deep zone, the linebackers can only cover the three or four underneath zones, so one short area is normally open. There are also two deep seams on either side of the middle safetyman (Diagram 2-37).
5. If the three deep secondary revolves or rolls to one side or the

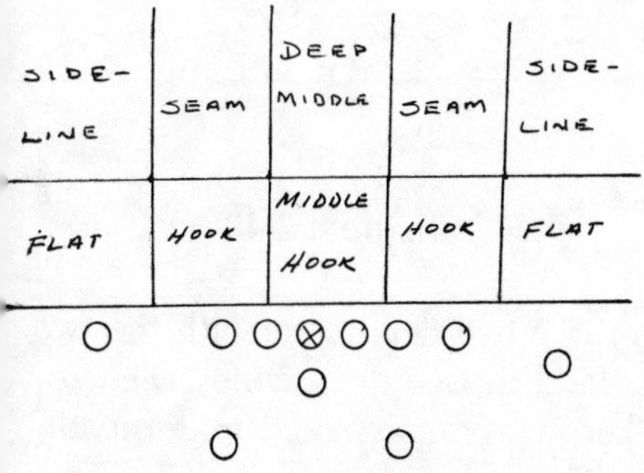

| SIDE-LINE | SEAM | DEEP MIDDLE | SEAM | SIDE-LINE |
|---|---|---|---|---|
| FLAT | HOOK | MIDDLE HOOK | HOOK | FLAT |

**Diagram 2-36**

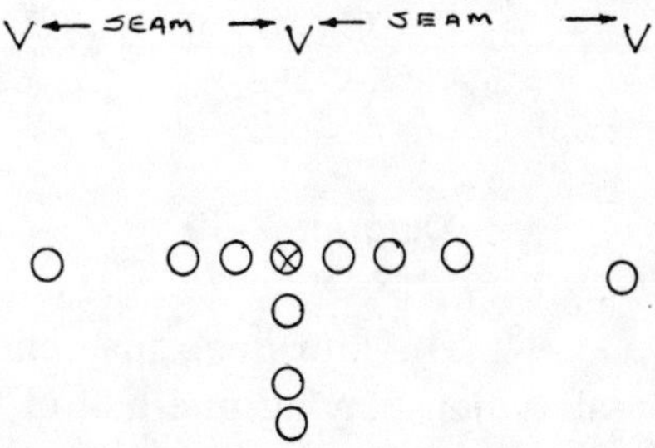

**Diagram 2-37**

other, the two deep sideline zones are open (Diagram 2-38). Now the four linebacker defense plus the rolling defensive back can cover all five underneath zones (Diagram 2-38).

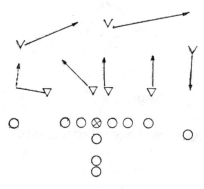

**Diagram 2-38**

*Four Deep Alignment:*

1. The four deep may be a straight man to man, often with a blitz by one or more linebackers (Diagram 2-39).
2. The four deep may be in a man-to-man coverage with a free safetyman.
3. The four deep may revolve to the strong or short side, where it becomes a three deep secondary (Diagram 2-40).

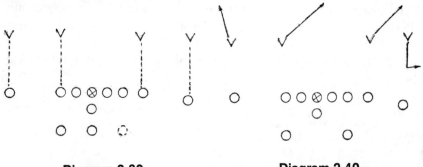

**Diagram 2-39**                       **Diagram 2-40**

4. The four deep may end up in a two deep zone with the two safetymen playing one-half of the field in two deep zones. The remaining cornerbacks and linebackers may be assigned underneath, man-to-man, or zone pass defense (Diagram 2-41).

5. Occasionally the four deep remains in a four deep zone, and three linebackers cover the underneath areas (usually on long yardage situations (Diagram 2-42).

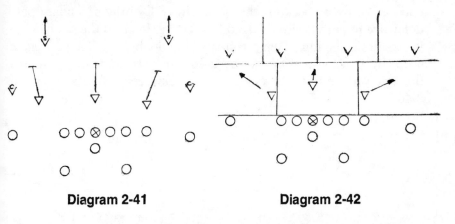

Diagram 2-41                                        Diagram 2-42

## The Quarterback's Pro Break Secondary Read

Whenever the quarterback sees the weakside safety (to the split end's side) in his #1 alignment or four-across-the-board look (Diagram 2-43), the quarterback is coached to immediately go to his double side attack. This means the quarterback calls in the huddle or on the line of scrimmage for both of the wide receivers to run their respective sideline cuts (Diagram 2-44).

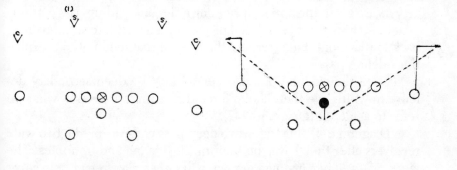

Diagram 2-43                                        Diagram 2-44

The quarterback is taught that if it is a four-across-the-board zone, the pass defense can roll only to one side of the formation, so the passer throws to the sideline receiver away from the secondary roll. Diagram 2-45 illustrates the defensive secondary rolling to the flanker's side, so the quarterback hits the split end with the sideline pass. The well-schooled quarterback knows that the defense normally rolls to the flanker (the two quick receivers' side), and thinks "split end" as he drops back for the pass. This roll of the secondary pass defensive pattern is also referred to as corner force. If the safety force is used from the four deep secondary, the double sideline pass again normally goes to the split end, because usually the defense again uses this safety force to the strong or two quick receivers' side (Diagram 2-46).

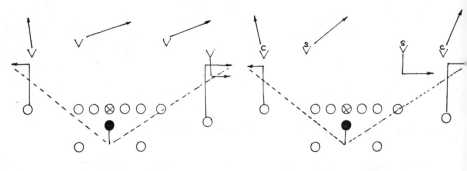

**Diagram 2-45**                              **Diagram 2-46**

If the four-across-the-board secondary is a four deep, man-to-man defense, the passer may throw the sideline pass to either wide receiver. Whenever the wide defensive cornerback overplays the sideline route in his man-to-man coverage technique, the wide receivers are given the option of running a sideline-and-up pass pattern. Whether this pass is completed or incompleted, it forces the cornerback to play honest and respect the deep threat, and not to overplay the sideline pass.

Once the sideline pass has spread out the deep secondary defense in width, we then like to force the secondary deep in what we refer to as depth (Diagram 2-47).

Diagram 2-47 illustrates two deep pass patterns by the two wide receivers after they have run their quick sideline-and-up routes. The weak safety, if playing man to man, will either play free or help cover the deep split end's cut (Diagram 2-48). If this happens, the quarterback reads the weak safety's free route and hits the tight end over the deep back's vacated area. If the safety is playing a straight, four-across-the-board, man-to-man defense, he will start out to the flat to play the swinging left running back on a man-to-man basis (Diagram 2-49). Again, the quarterback may throw to hit the crossing tight end

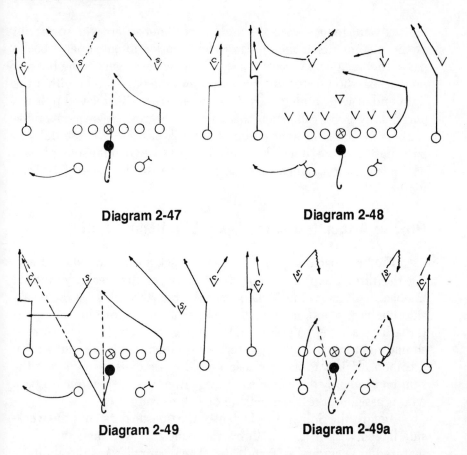

**Diagram 2-47**                    **Diagram 2-48**

**Diagram 2-49**                    **Diagram 2-49a**

as we saw in Diagram 2-48, or he may throw deep to the split end who has drawn single man-to-man coverage by the split side defensive cornerback. As shown in Diagrams 2-47 and 2-48, the flankerback is coached to run a post cut, since the strongside safety is assigned to cover the tight end man-to-man. The flanker begins his side-and-up route, but changes to a deep post cut when the strong safety takes off. The flankerback, drawing single coverage, is another optional deep receiving threat.

Since the deep secondary defenders are now cognizant of the deep and wide passing threat of the two wide receivers, the third pass selection versus the four-across-the-board defensive secondary is the Delay Pass. The delay pass runs both the left running back and tight end on their set, block-delayed pass routes. Once the deep defensive backs begin to sprint backward to stop the deep or the wide pass patterns, they are now forced to regroup and begin to attack the delayed receiver (Diagram 2-49a). These delayed pass patterns are most advantageous versus the undercover linebackers who sprint out of the alignments to get greater depth prior to the quarterback's pass. The delayed pass is also a successful weapon versus the blitzing linebacker who vacates his area and allows the passer to hit either the tight end or left running back in this open area. The delayed pass is a particularly good call when the offense features two maneuverable runners in both the tight end and tailback positions. These delayed pass patterns are normal routes for these two offensive players whenever their assigned defenders do not rush the passer (Diagram 2-50).

## How to Attack the Three Deep Eight Man Front

The first coaching point the quarterback must learn when attacking the three deep, eight man front is to key the weakside outside linebacker. Against the 53 Defense, the quarterback keys the weakside linebacker and, as soon as the linebacker rushes him, the quarterback passes the ball off to the swinging tailback. If the linebacker should run to the flat, the quarterback is taught to hit the split end on a comeback pass route, because now the passer is assured that the split end can only draw single coverage from the deep defensive back who is assigned the deep outside one-third zone.

Against the Split-Forty Defense, the quarterback keys the weakside linebacker, or he may throw the same passes to the split side as featured in Diagrams 2-50 and 2-51. The passer also has the ability to throw to the strong side. The flanker runs a curl, and the tight end runs an arrow cut. We call these combined routes a "Carol" cut. Since

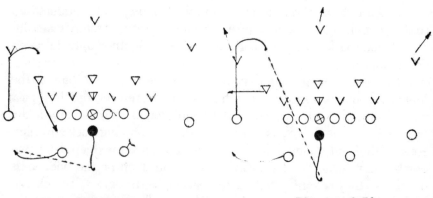

Diagram 2-50                              Diagram 2-51

the three deep pass defense requires the deep outside defender to cover the deep outside one-third zone, he has to overplay either the curl or the arrow cut. The passer can hit either of the open receivers. The right running back sets to block, starts a swing pass pattern to force the outside strong linebacker to move to the flat, then cuts upfield to prevent the inside strongside Split-Forty linebacker from helping out on the Carol route (Diagram 2-52).

Another method of attacking the Split-Forty is to attack the area vacated by the two inside split linebackers. Diagram 2-53 illustrates the drop-back passer checking the strong side with the two quick strong-side receivers running their Carol route, while the strongside running back is coached to fake a block and loop and hook into the zone directly over the offensive center's original position. The tight

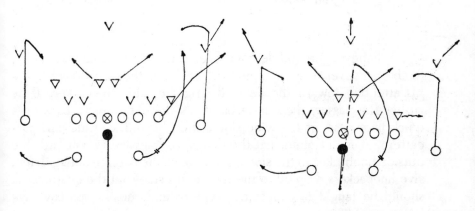

Diagram 2-52          Diagram 2-53

end and the strongside running back have the ability to exchange assignments, which calls for the tight end to run the middle hook route, while the running back runs his arrow course (Diagram 2-54).

If the weak or split side and middle linebackers begin to drop off, favoring the strong side of the formation, the quarterback keys the middle linebacker and throws opposite the coverage of the middle linebacker. This means the passer throws to the tight end running his post cut into the seam between the overshifted middle safety and the outside deep left defensive back covering his deep outside one-third zone. The right running back also checks the coverage of the left outside linebacker. If the outside linebacker to the tight end's side drops off into his normal flat coverage assignment, the right running back loops into the open area between this defender and the middle linebacker, who is favoring the two wide receivers' side (Diagram 2-55).

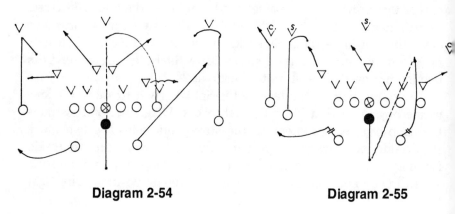

**Diagram 2-54**                    **Diagram 2-55**

Whenever the middle linebacker and the left defensive outside linebacker cover away from the twin receivers, the quarterback forces his attention toward the defensive right outside linebacker. If he rushes the passer, the quarterback hits the left running back on a quick flare pass, or the wide slotback on his quick inside curl pass pattern. It is not often that the defensive linebackers will rush the outside linebacker to the slot side and have the two remaining defensive linebackers drop off to the tight end's side, but the quarterback should be taught to expect this type of underneath pass coverage (Diagram 2-56).

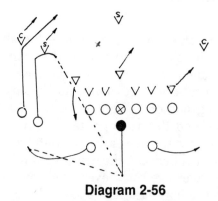

**Diagram 2-56**

The Pro Break Right Formation helps to spread out the two deep five underneath zone pass defense. The two wide receivers are as-

signed to run their respective flag pass patterns, because the deep
outside zones are open areas since the two deep pass defenders must
cover their respective one-half zones. As soon as the ball is snapped
and the quarterback drops back to show "pass," the five underneath
defenders are assigned to cover the five underneath zones. The two
set offensive backs check their blocks and flare out into the vacated
flats, looking for the ball in these open flat areas. The fifth potential
receiver is the tight end, who is instructed to slow block the defender
over him and run under control down the middle, into the hole. The
hole is located just beyond the middle linebacker's zone and the
middle of the twin safetys' original alignment positions (Diagram
2-57).

If the outside linebacker over the offensive tight end blitzes, the
tight end should continue running straight upfield and look for a quick
pass. The passer is coached to hit the tight end in the numbers, and
the receiver is taught to look for the pass over his inside shoulder. The
tight end's route must be run straight upfield, not toward the inside.
If the receiver bends his route toward the inside, he may run into the
middle linebacker's zone (Diagram 2-58).

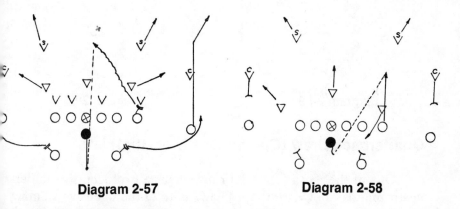

| Diagram 2-57 | Diagram 2-58 |

## The Quarterback Draw
## Featuring Inside Fold Blocking

The Quarterback Draw is one of the more difficult draws to stop
in football. This draw gives the offense an extra offensive player to
block a defender at the point of the attack or to influence a particular
defender away from the point of the attack.

The quarterback is coached to take a three-step drop (right-left-
right) resembling his normal drop-back pass route, then plant his back

(right) foot and break for daylight up the middle. This three-step timing gives the quarterback just enough time to allow his blockers to take their proper blocking angles, and gives the linebackers just enough time to take the bait. Once the linebackers see an apparent pass play, they begin their backward drops; at that moment, the "pseudo-passer" plants his back foot and begins to charge forward on his draw play. One of the most difficult maneuvers for a linebacker is to change gears after starting backwards to shuffle up to a balanced position and begin to move forward and re-react to a particular offensive maneuver.

When attacking the 52 Defense, as illustrated in Diagram 2-59, the outside tackles employ an inside fold blocking technique and go downfield in search of the 52 inside linebackers. Normally, in a passing situation, the Oklahoma linebackers are scurrying back to their respective hook zones (Diagram 2-60).

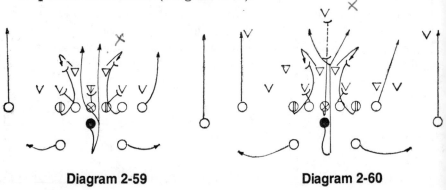

Diagram 2-59                                  Diagram 2-60

## Quarterback Draw (One-on-One Blocking)

One of the most successful runs versus a two deep five underneath zone is the Quarterback Draw. Both of the offensive running backs flare to their respective sides, drawing the inside underneath defenders wide. The quarterback is coached to drop back three steps, plant, and run directly at the offensive center. The quarterback is taught to cut off the center's block on the defensive middle guard (Diagram 2-61).

All of the offensive linemen drop back as if to set up for their pocket protection, then fire out on their assigned defenders. The outside receiver uses deep run-off pass routes, and the tight end runs his arrow cut to draw the pass defenders away from the quarterback's draw (point of the attack).

## Halfback Flag Pass

The Halfback Flag Pass is called by the quarterback whenever the defensive safetyman hangs in his position to the split end's side. If a linebacker attempts to defend against the halfback, the back merely outruns the linebacker. If the defensive safety revolves over quickly, the halfback is taught to run a deep fly pass pattern (dotted line in Diagram 2-62). The quick ride fake to the backside running back often holds the defenders just long enough for the pass receivers to break clear for the long bomb.

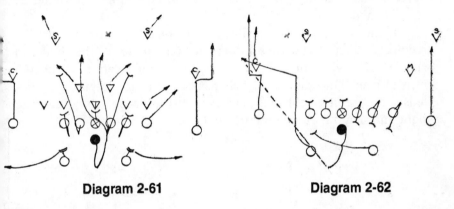

Diagram 2-61                        Diagram 2-62

## Veer Counter Bootleg Pass

Two quick dive fakes by the quarterback precede the bootleg action and a pass to the frontside running back (Diagram 2-63). A quick weak fake to the backside set back helps the frontside running back to get through the line and free into the flat. The quarterback makes a strong fake to the backside running back, bootlegs to the

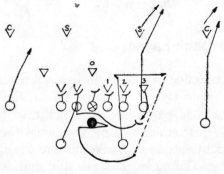

Diagram 2-63

strong side, and hits the frontside running back about four yards deep in the flat. The key pass protection block is assigned to the backside offensive guard. He is assigned to pull shallow along the line of scrimmage and gain depth to pick up the strongside #3 defender.

## Pro Curl Tight Swing

The straight drop-back pass calls for the split end to run his curl pass route. If the strong safetyman takes the flat and the strong cornerback takes the deep one-third area, the Twin split end should be open (Diagram 2-64).

If the secondary is playing a man-to-man defense on the Pro receiver, the split end runs a deep curl pass pattern. The tight end runs a wide swing route which forces the strong safety to cover him man-to-man (Diagram 4-64). When playing a man-to-man pass defense, the curling split end may pick off the inside safety, and the tight end may break free on his swing cut.

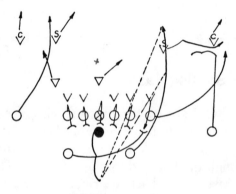

Diagram 2-64

## Quick Post Throwback Pass

Whenever the backside outside right linebacker starts to overpursue toward the Triple Option's running threat, the Quick Post Throwback Pass is a good pass call. The quick dive by the right running back and the quarterback's Triple Option fake action help to draw this backside right outside linebacker toward the apparent Triple Option maneuver. The passer hits the split end as soon as he breaks clear. If the left split end is not open, the quarterback is instructed to look for the left running back, who is assigned to run a crease pattern between the middle safetyman and the strongside safetyman (Diagram 2-65).

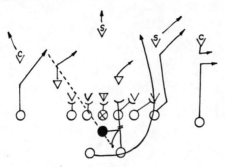

**Diagram 2-65**

Chapter 3 deals with the hard-hitting Power-I Offense. The Power I's sweep, off tackle, isolation, and counter plays are discussed against many different defensive sets. The success of this powerful goal line offense is also covered in depth in the next chapter. This attack resembles the powerful, old Single-Wing Formation, with the addition of the modern Power-I backfield shifts, which offer this formation an explosive, balanced running and passing attack.

# 3

# THE POWER-I OFFENSE

## How the Power-I Offense Will Help You to Win

The Power I is an excellent short yardage offense. It is one of the most successful offensive attacks used to score on the goal line attack. Its power resembles the old Single Wing Formation, featuring the power halfback as the lead or extra blocker at the point of the attack. Because of the unique backfield alignment, a counter play may be run, faking to a back in one direction and utilizing a lead back blocking at the point of the attack.

Originally the Power-I attack was unbalanced to the halfback's side; but with the modern halfback shift, the Power I has become a more explosive formation. Motion has also given the Power I a new look. Long halfback motion to the tight end's side gives the formation a Pro "look." Long halfback motion to the split end's side gives the formation a Twin "look." Tailback motion is another method of changing the face of the Power-I "look."

The basic Power I gives the quarterback an excellent sprint-out path away from the halfback, to the opposite side of the formation. The faking potential of the three-back set lends itself to play-action passes. The sprint-out pass gives the quarterback a three-back lead-blocking potential, or a quick flood pass route using the lead backs as possible receivers.

## The Advantages of the Power-I Attack

1. Just as the name implies, this formation is designed to overpower the defense with a consistent ground attack.

2. A quick shift helps to give the Power I a balanced power attack to either side of the offensive line.

3. The three-back set helps to fake the defense out of position as well as to block the defense for power thrusts.

4. Motion by the power halfback away from the split end gives the formation a new Pro-I "look."

5. This formation lends itself to the explosive Triple Option attack.

6. The Counter Play has added emphasis with a faking back going in one direction and the ball carrier, escorted by a lead blocker, moving in the opposite direction.

7. Successful sprint-out passes should be emphasized because of the alignment of the offensive power backfield.

8. The tailback has the opportunity to hit any hole along the line of scrimmage from his deep I alignment.

9. No new goal line plays need to be practiced, because the Power I's normal running attack is the same attack as featured on the goal line.

10. A strong running quarterback gives this formation another potential scoring threat.

11. Play-action passes are successful because of the three-man faking ability of the Power I.

12. Isolation plays have been consistent gainers from this three-back set.

13. Sprint-out option plays have a lead back to make this series more explosive from the Power-I formation.

14. Two-man kick-out blocks add to the success of the off tackle power plays.

## Requirements for the Power-I Personnel

*Tailback*—The tailback should be a big, strong, durable runner who has the ability to run to either side of the formation. He should be selected primarily as a ball carrier.

*Fullback*—Blocking ability is the most important attribute that the fullback must possess. The fullback's normal ball carrying assignments should be limited to quick-hitting inside running plays.

*Halfbacks*—Lead, power, and isolation blocking techniques must be mastered by the power halfback. He must be strong and durable enough to help double team block with the fullback. The halfback should also possess pass-receiving ability.

*Quarterback*—Ball handling is the most important item for the quarterback. The quarterback should be an adequate passer and a good, strong power runner.

*Split End*—He should be selected based upon his ability to make the "Big Catch." He should have speed and be able to execute the crack-back block.

*Tight End*—This end should be big enough to make the power double team block and fast enough to get free to catch the ball.

*Interior Five Linemen*—The blocking five should be big enough and heavy enough to blow the defensive front off the line of scrimmage. Since this offensive attack is based upon power, all five of these blockers must be able to execute the power double team block. Thus, fire-out techniques must be perfected by these interior offensive line blockers.

## Power-I Formation's Alignment

The fullback lines up directly behind the center, four and one-half yards deep. He uses a three- or four-point stance, and is used primarily as a blocker. The tailback lines up approximately five and one-half yards deep, directly behind the fullback. A two-point stance is used by the I-back. A three-point stance is used by the halfback, who is coached to line up four and one-half yards deep. His normal alignment should split the inside leg of the offensive tackle. At times his alignment may vary from directly behind the offensive tackle to splitting the outside leg of the tackle. The specific alignment of the halfback depends on the play called by the quarterback (Diagram 3-1).

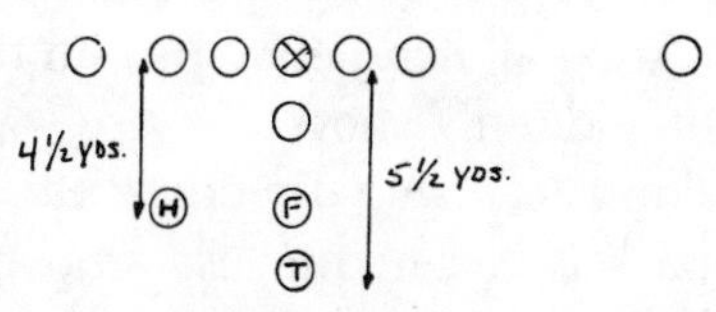

**Diagram 3-1**

## The Power-I Sweep

The Power-I Sweep emphasizes this formation's ability to turn the corner of the opposition's defense. Once the power attack has established this prerequisite, the inside power thrusts become a more explosive threat to the defense with each succeeding play.

The Power Sweep does not always have the ability to turn the defensive corner, because it often turns into an off tackle play. The ball carrier has the option running assignment of cutting upfield, inside, or outside the defensive corner—whenever he sees daylight.

The offensive line's blocking assignments are described in the following manner:

### Power Sweep Linemen's Assignments

| | |
|---|---|
| Split End | — Walk-away linebacker, Monster, deep back your side. |
| Frontside Tackle | — Drive inside man. |
| Frontside Guard | — Fold or hook the man on or outside the tackle. |
| Center | — Block #0, frontside gap, backside. |
| Backside Guard | — Inside gap, pull and lead play. |
| Backside Tackle | — Pull inside—cut off. |
| Backside End | — Crossfield shallow in front of the point of attack. |

The Power Sweep's offensive linemen's assignments, as discussed above, describe how all seven offensive line blockers are able to block any given opponent's defense. Diagram 3-2 illustrates the linemen's blocking assignments against the Oklahoma 52 Defense.

A reverse pivot on the frontside foot by the quarterback begins the power sweep. This allows the quarterback to make his reverse pivot and a two-handed pitch to the left halfback. The quarterback stays off the line of scrimmage to allow the backside guard to pull and clear for him. Then, the ball handler steps into the line to seal off any defender who might suddenly show.

The fullback takes a lead step directly at the outside hip of the #3 defender. The fullback is coached to use an overthrow block on the #3 defender. If the #3 defender is in a stacked position, the blocker must block the defender who shows in the #3 area. Against a gap eight defense, the fullback is assigned to hook block the #4 defender (Diagram 3-3).

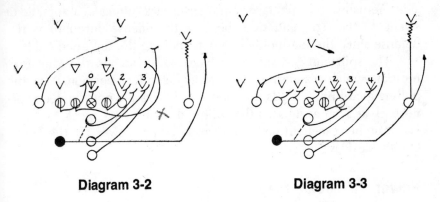

Diagram 3-2                                    Diagram 3-3

The tailback blocks the first defender to show outside of the fullback's lead block. Against the Gap Eight Defense, the tailback should look inside first to pick off the middle safetyman.

A lead step by the ball carrier (left halfback) puts him in position to receive the quarterback's pitch-out. The ball carrier is coached to run on a path parallel to the line of scrimmage, and to make the play appear to be a wide sweep. At the last moment, the ball carrier is taught to cut off the lead blocks of the fullback and the tailback.

Diagram 3-4 illustrates the Power Sweep against the 44 Defense. The frontside guard uses his fold block and picks up the quick scrapping linebacker on the line of scrimmage. A key block versus the 44 Defense is performed by the tailback, as he is assigned to block the #4 defender, who is the first defender outside of the fullback's assignment.

Diagram 3-5 shows the Power Sweep in action against the 52 Gap

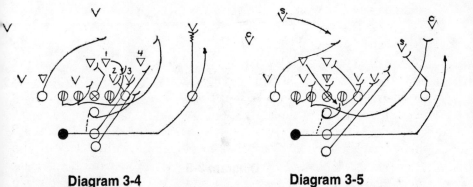

Diagram 3-4                                    Diagram 3-5

Stacked Defense. With the middle guard stacked to the split end side, the power sweep is still effective to the middle guard's stacked side. Actually we would favor our quarterback calling an automatic to sweep to the tight end side, because the offense outnumbers the defense since there are only five defenders to the tight end's side.

The split end is assigned to block a defender in the Monster's position, which is a glorified walk-away defender's position. Now the pulling guard pulls, leads the play, and blocks the outside deep cornerback as soon as he sees the split end's crack-back block.

Another excellent power play used by the Power I is the Power Off Tackle Play.

## Power Off Tackle Play

The Power Off Tackle Play is one of the most important running plays in the Power-I offensive attack. The two kick-out blockers, plus the backside guard's pulling lead block, help to assist the all-important double team power block at the point of the attack.

Diagram 3-6 illustrates this power play to the tight end's side against the basic Oklahoma Defense. The tailback (ball carrier) is taught to take a lead step, then a cross-over step, push off his foot, and drive directly for the hole. The ball carrier is coached to favor the double team block by running as close to this power block as possible. All of the key blocks at the point of the attack should be explained to the tailback so he can make an intelligent cut for daylight once he drives into the hole.

The Power Off Tackle's blocking assignments are discussed in detail below; they will guide the reader in blocking any given defense (Diagram 3-6).

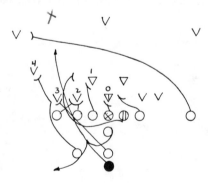

**Diagram 3-6**

## Power Off Tackle's Assignments

| | |
|---|---|
| Split End | — Block deep middle one-third. |
| Backside Tackle | — Inside cut-off |
| Backside Guard | — Pull, cut upfield close to the power block, look to the inside, and seal off inside pursuit. |
| Center | — Block #0; if no #0, block backside. |
| Frontside Guard | — Block #1 away from the point of attack. |
| Frontside Tackle | — Block inside gap; if none, post #2. If #2 lines up inside, drive block #2. |
| Frontside End | — Block first man inside. |
| Halfback | — Influence #3 and block #4 outside. |
| Fullback | — Run an inside-out course and kick out #3 defender. (Against a gap defense, kick out #4 if the end drives on #3). |
| Tailback | — Take three steps, receive the ball, and make your cut upfield—cut for daylight. |

Blocking the 44 Defense may be done in two ways. In Diagram 3-7, the frontside guard and tackle block their assigned defenders because the frontside guard is able to get a good angle on the #1 linebacker. However, if the #1 linebacker's alignment is nearer the point of the attack (possibly stacked behind the defensive frontside tackle #2), the fold block may have to be called.

Diagram 3-8 demonstrates how the fold block looks versus the 44 Defense.

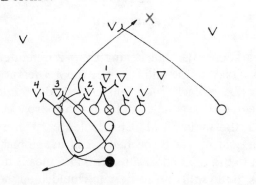 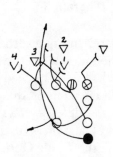

**Diagram 3-7**                    **Diagram 3-8**

Against a gap goal line defense, the fullback's assignment calls for him to kick out on the #4 defender if the tight end blocks down on the #3 man (Diagram 3-9). This means both the lead halfback and the fullback block out on the #4 defender versus the Gap Eight Defense.

## Power I's Triple Option

The Triple Option is an exciting play from the Power I's attack. The halfback may be shifted from left to right halfback or vice versa. The key to the success of this play is that the tailback is always the pitch-back. This means the same man is the lead back, dive back, and pitchman on all Triple Option plays! The tailback is also closer to the corner, whether he is running the Triple Option play to his left or to his right.

Diagram 3-10 illustrates the Triple Option play to the split end's side, with the lead halfback set to this side after a shift from his previous right halfback's set position. This shift takes place a split second before the snap of the ball. Against the 61 Defense, the #2 defender tackles the fullback and the #3 man attacks the quarterback.

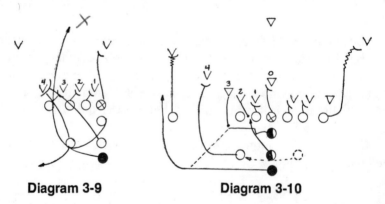

| Diagram 3-9 | Diagram 3-10 |

Therefore, the quarterback keeps the ball, keying the #2 defender first; then he pitches the ball back to the tailback once the #3 defender attacks him. The lead halfback blocks the Monster defender while the split end runs off the deep wide secondary defender (cornerback).

If the defense stays in the same 52 Monster Defense, as illustrated in Diagram 3-10, our quarterback is coached to call an automatic to run the Triple Option to the tight end's side. This also means he would not shift his halfback to the split end's side, but would keep the halfback in his normal right halfback position (Diagram 3-11).

Diagram 3-11 shows the extra blocker (right halfback) looking to the inside, leading the ball carrier wide around the corner. If the defense decides to put the #2 man on the quarterback instead of the fullback, the quarterback is coached to hand the ball off to the fullback. But, since the #2 defender closes down on the fullback and the #3 defender attacks the quarterback, the pitch-out is executed, as pointed out in the diagram.

## Tailback Isolation Play

When attacking up the "pike" versus the Split Forty Defense, the Power I attacks the strong inside linebacker. The frontside guard at the point of the attack is taught to take a maximum split from the center to help isolate the linebacker to the guard's inside. The frontside guard, tackle, and tight end turn out on the defenders to their outside. The center blocks back on the backside split linebacker. The backside guard and tackle block back or turn out on the defenders to their respective outside areas (Diagram 3-12).

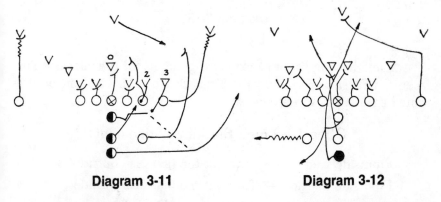

Diagram 3-11                              Diagram 3-12

The I-tailback is coached to take a drop step with his right foot and fire straight for the inside foot of the frontside (left) offensive guard. He must lift his inside elbow up to accept the ball from the quarterback and follow the fullback. The I-back is instructed to cut off the head-on isolated block by the lead offensive fullback. The fullback takes off on a straight course for the inside right split linebacker and is coached to drive his forehead directly through the defender's numbers, running right over the linebacker. A deep reverse pivot is executed by the quarterback, then the ball handler continues down the line (toward the tight end), faking his potential option play.

When running the Tailback Isolation Play at the seven man front Oklahoma 52 Defense, the left guard also takes a maximum split to help isolate the right 52 inside linebacker. The tight end, strong tackle, center, split guard, and tackle block their one-on-one blocking assignments. Only the strong or frontside offensive guard blocks on a different angle, and he is assigned to drive block the #0 nose defender, who has been posted by the center. The split end blocks the deep middle-one-third area, and all of the backs carry out their same play assignments as illustrated in Diagram 3-12. Diagram 3-13 illustrates the isolation against the Oklahoma Defense.

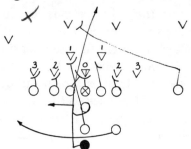

**Diagram 3-13**

The following list of blocking assignments for the offensive linemen is written concisely so the Tailback Isolation Play can be executed against any given defense.

### Offensive Line's Blocking Assignments

| | |
|---|---|
| Frontside End | — Turn out the first man outside. |
| Frontside Tackle | — Turn out the first man outside. |
| Frontside Guard | — #0; if no one there, #1 on line |
| Center | — #0; if no one there, #1 backside |
| Backside Guard | — #1 |
| Backside Tackle | — Turn out the first man outside. |
| Backside End | — Middle one-third. |

## Power-I Counter

The Counter off the Power I is a solid ground gainer, particularly versus the quick-flowing Oklahoma linebackers. The offensive frontside tackle is assigned to turn out on the defensive tackle. He must hold this block long enough for the quarterback to make his offside fake to the fullback, reverse, and hand the ball off to the tailback. The frontside guard drives down and double teams the nose guard. If the posting center is able to block the #0 defender by himself, the frontside guard is instructed to recognize this and to release, continue to the second phase of his co-op block, and pick off the backside defensive linebacker. The co-op block means that the frontside blocking guard co-operates with the center and either helps him double team the middle guard or turns upfield and picks off the backside linebacker (Diagram 3-14).

## Power-I Counter Trap

The Power-I Counter Trap is a combination of a trap and a lead back torpedo play. The quarterback makes a quick fake to the fullback over the offensive left guard. The left offensive guard pulls and kicks out or traps the defensive #2 man. The double combo block is assigned to the center as the post man and the right guard as the drive man. The right tackle sets the defensive #2 man, then turns out on the #3 defender. The tailback leads and torpedoes the frontside #1 defender; the left halfback takes the hand-off and cuts off the tailback's torpedo isolation block (Diagram 3-15).

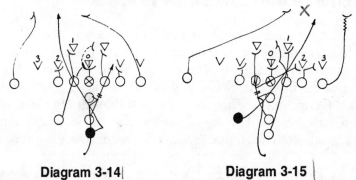

Diagram 3-14        Diagram 3-15

## Quarterback Counter

The Quarterback Counter Play means that the quarterback goes opposite the flow of the other offensive backs. Whenever this play has been called, the ball carrier is coached to look for daylight and cut up quickly into this open area. This play is not only an offensive long gainer but it is an offensive maneuver that keeps the backside interior defenders honest. This means the backside interior defenders cannot overpursue toward the initial move of the quarterback or the flow of the offensive backs.

After the quarterback makes his initial move, he is taught to push off his back foot, tuck the ball into his "third hand" (stomach), and wrap both hands around the ball. This play must be run live and at full speed so the ball carrier can read the defensive flow. This is particularly true when facing the 44 Defense (Diagram 3-16).

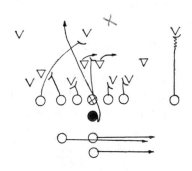

**Diagram 3-16**

## The Power I's Goal Line Offensive Attack

Selling our offense the belief that they can score whenever they reach the opposition's ten yard line is the most important objective of a consistent scoring offense. The success of our goal line attack is based upon the front line blocker's ability to eliminate penetration by the goal line defenders. Therefore, the goal line scoring plays, along with emphasizing the key cut-off and wedge-blocking techniques, must be practiced in each practice session throughout the entire season.

The offensive psychological approach is that the odds are with the offense, because it knows in advance the one or possibly two defensive alignments the opponent's will use. While the offense has the element of surprise on its side, it may also choose from any number of formations and run or pass plays.

A great deal of importance in scouting and game film reports is directed toward the alignment, techniques, and secondary's assignment in the opposition's defense. From these reports, we design the game plan for our offensive goal line attack.

## Power I Versus Gap Eight Goal Line Defense

Once inside the ten yard line, the strength of the goal line offense is its powerful blocking unit. Therefore, a tight formation is often most advantageous down near the opposition's goal line. This tight formation, the Power I, is designed to drive the football across the goal line. The quarterback is taught first to attack the off tackle area whenever the opposition lines up in their gap eight goal line defense (Diagram 3-17).

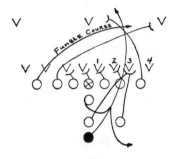

**Diagram 3-17**

Both of the guards, the center, and the playside tackle block back on the gap defenders. The frontside halfback and upback in the Power I double team the defensive #3 man to the outside. The defensive middle safetyman is eliminated by the frontside end's across-field block. The backside tackle runs his shallow across-field path, aiming at the farside defensive safetyman. The left offensive end takes a slightly deeper course than the backside tackle because the end's assignment is the "fumble route." The fumble route means that the backside end runs his across-field route, looking for a possible fumble by the ball carrier. The reason we have incorporated the fumble course is that the gap goal line defenses are very aggressive, and are often successful in pulling or clawing the ball loose from the ball carrier.

The quarterback is taught to hand the ball off to the running back deep in the backfield. The reasoning behind the deep hand-off is that we do not want to take any chances of handing off too close to the line of scrimmage, because we are attacking a gap eight defense whose main objective is to penetrate and create a fumble or loss of yardage. Another reason for the deep hand-off is to allow the tailback the chance to alter his course to where there is a defensive opening.

Actually, we would like our ball carrier to run the "picture play" as demonstrated in Diagram 3-17, but the ball carrier has the option of running for daylight if an opening exists in a different area.

The quarterback is coached to continue to fake wide to hold the defensive end, keeping the #4 man from closing down on the ball carrier. Against the 65 Goal Line Defense, the offense isolates the second defender outside of the center and sends the two offensive backs to torpedo block the #2 defender (Diagram 3-18).

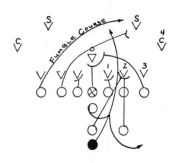

**Diagram 3-18**

## Power I Against the 65 Goal Line Defense

When attacking the 65 Defense on the goal line, the offensive guard is taught to block his inside gap, driving his shoulder in front of the defender and stepping with his inside foot first. The playside end blocks down on the middle linebacker, just as he did on the safetyman versus the Gap Eight Defense. The playside tackle drop-steps and blocks out on the defensive end. His course has a tendency to hold or cause the defender, who is to be double teamed, to take a check step to his outside, mirroring the offensive tackle's outside route. The center reaches for the middle linebacker, attacking where the defender will be rather than his position prior to the snap of the ball.

The backside guard is assigned to cut off the defender to his inside, while the backside tackle takes his shallow across-field course. Again, the backside end runs his fumble course, with an easy chance for a touchdown if a fumble should occur.

The running back has a greater chance of cutting this play back over the middle because the offense is running one hole closer to the center against the 65 Defense. Thus, constantly make sure that the ball carrier always hits the point of attack with his shoulders parallel to the line of scrimmage. This technique gives the runner more forward thrust and power as he drives straight into the line.

## The Wedge Attack

A straight-ahead attack is a must near the goal line. To meet defensive power, the attack uses its favorite power weapon—the Wedge. The offensive man selected as the apex of the wedge is the #2 defender. The two men on each side of our lead blocker point their eyes at our apex man's hip and drive forward. Blockers who use the wedge-blocking techniques must always keep their feet; for once the blockers lose their feet, the wedge becomes useless (Diagram 3-19).

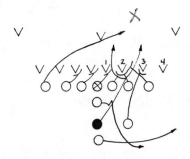

**Diagram 3-19**

The blocking technique of the apex of the wedge is to fire out, raise both arms shoulder high, hit into the man over him, use short choppy steps, and drive the defender upward and backward. If no man is over the blocker, he should fire out and drive inside into the defender's body, keeping his legs chopping.

All of the other linemen are taught to block down the line, bringing up the arms into the double forearm position. Each lineman should put his helmet across and in front of the hip of his teammate. Each blocker must make sure that no defender gets between him and the next blocker. The blocker must not lose his balance; he should keep his feet pumping all the time.

## Fullback Wedge Play

The Fullback Wedge off the Power I combines quick-hitting and power. The fullback is coached to aim directly at the apex of the wedge and break slightly to the left or right if he sees an opening. If no opening appears, the fullback should blast straight ahead, keeping his feet driving and maintaining his balance until the wedge breaks down.

The center and right end pinch ahead to cut off the first defend-ers outside of the wedge. The cut-off blocker may have to scramble into blocking position on all fours, if he must, to cut off the opponent. The frontside halfback also strikes a path to cut off the defensive tackle so that he cannot close down and hit the fullback from a side-angle approach. Cut-off blocks are also used by both the backside guard and tackle, making sure each scrambles with his head in front of the defender. The backside end again runs his fumble course.

The quarterback opens up by stepping back with his right foot on a forty-five degree angle and slightly riding the fullback into the line. The open hand-off is used so as not to force the ball carrier too wide by coaching the quarterback to use his reverse pivot. The tailback sprints right on his wide sweep route.

## The Quarterback Wedge Sneak

The Quarterback Wedge Sneak is another must play in the goal line offense's repertoire. There are many times when a team needs a yard or less; the Quarterback Wedge Sneak offers a limited amount of ball handling and a quick middle thrust that assures consistent short yardage gains.

The Quarterback Wedge Sneak with more than five yards to go on an early down is an intelligent call, using a quick snap count. It not only takes the defense by surprise, but it also keeps the middle of the opposition's defense tight with the constant threat of the wedge sneak. Whenever the opponent strengthens his interior defense, he leaves other defensive areas weakened.

The quarterback is taught to delay slightly, then aim into the opened area with his legs driving and his shoulder low. It is the second and third effort by our quarterback that makes this play suc-cessful. The signal caller should not immediately push into the cen-ter's tail, as this often forces the quarterback into an upright position, taking away a great deal of his forward momentum.

The Quarterback Wedge should be used near the goal line, mov-ing the apex out and away from the center whenever the defense is setting up a special goal line defense to stop the wedge.

## Quarterback's Run-Pass Option

On third or fourth down and more than three yards to go for a touchdown or a first down inside the opposition's ten yard line, the Quarterback's Run-Pass Option Play is a good call (Diagram 3-20). All of the offensive linemen use their reach-blocking techniques on this play.

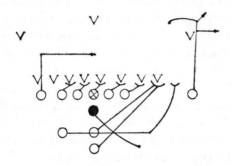

**Diagram 3-20**

Reach-blocking techniques are used when the defensive man has outside position on the blocker. The offense should move the defender off the line of scrimmage and force the defender to turn his shoulders perpendicular to the line of scrimmage, consequently forcing the defender to take a poor pursuit course. The blocker should explode off the line of scrimmage, stepping with the near foot, dropping his tail low, and hitting the defender on the rise. The blocker must keep his head up and stay on his feet. To force the defender off the line of scrimmage, the blocker may have to ground his hands and go into the four-point scramble blocking method. The blocker should not go into the four-point scrambling position until he has made solid contact with the defensive man. The blocker should aim his eyes at the defender's belt buckle to force the pursuing lineman to bring his hands down, giving the quarterback a clear picture of his receivers if he chooses to pass.

The blocker should be coached to reach for the outside knee of the defender, stepping with the frontside foot. The first step should be short, in the direction of where the defender will be rather than where the defender is before the snap of the ball. The blocker should keep his momentum forward, always fighting upfield. Reach blocking must consist of a second and third effort by the blocker, keeping his feet driving until the final whistle.

The run or pass option should be run from both the Power-I and the Slot-I formations. In Diagram 3-20, we run from the Power-I Formation against a Gap Eight Defense. The center and frontside guard and tackle reach out and block the nearest defender to their outside. The halfback reaches out on the defensive end and has double team help from the fullback, who sets a course for the outside knee of the defensive end. The tailback runs a wide course just outside the defensive end and picks up the first defender to show.

The quarterback sprints out with the thought of "run, first, and pass, second." If he is forced into passing, he looks first for the right end and second for the left end sprinting across the middle. The quarterback is coached to always throw—to throw on the run, sprinting upfield with his shoulders parallel to the line of scrimmage.

The backside end runs his across pattern, and if the quarterback decides to run, he continues on his fumble course. The split end to the halfback's side runs one of three patterns: a hook, sideline, or a flag cut. On all three of these patterns he sprints downfield ten yards, driving the secondary defender backward. These patterns help to open up the possibility of the run for the quarterback. The specific pass pattern is determined by the reaction of the outside safety defender.

Against a gap eight defense, our crossing backside end may become the primary receiver if the defensive secondary stays in their three deep coverage, with the split end stretching out the secondary's alignment (Diagram 3-20).

The Sprint-Out Run or Pass Option versus the 65 Goal Line Defense also calls for reach blocking by most of the offensive linemen. The main reach blocking rule for the blockers is to reach block on the man to the outside *if* you can *reach* him.

Against the 65 Defense, the right end posts the defensive tackle because the defensive end is too wide to reach. Therefore, we end up double teaming the defensive tackle, as the right offensive tackle reaches and becomes a drive man on this defender (Diagram 3-21). The offense knows the defense will be in a man-to-man coverage, because of the previous film's breakdown and scouting reports, and will try to run off the outside safetyman with the right end and force the middle safetyman to contain the sprint-out.

Motion is used only if the offense knows exactly how the defense will react to it. If the defense has more than one way to cover motion,

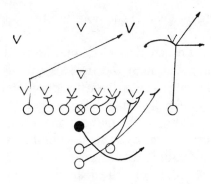

**Diagram 3-21**

the offense will neglect this offensive maneuver. Therefore, motion will be used only when it puts the defense in jeopardy.

## Off Tackle Power Play

The Off Tackle Power Play is used offensively to stretch the defensive perimeter by beginning to sweep wide, then cutting back off tackle. The two blocking backs kick the defensive end out and the ball carrier cuts up inside the double team block. Leading the ball carrier through the hole is the quarterback, who, after he pitches, sprints close to the line of scrimmage prior to turning upfield. Against a Gap Eight Defense (Diagram 3-22), all of the playside linemen block back to cut off the gap defenders.

Against the 65 Goal Line Defense (Diagram 3-23), the attack is able to get a double team block on, not only the defensive end, but also on the defensive #2 man. The offense wants the posting offensive tackle and the driving end to drive the defensive tackle backward on a

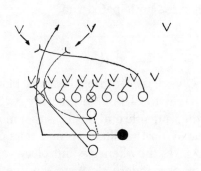

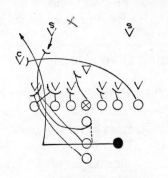

**Diagram 3-22**                              **Diagram 3-23**

forty-five degree angle to widen the hole and to cut off the defensive pursuit.

The ball carrier is coached to sprint on a straight line, parallel to the line of scrimmage, through the fullback's or up back's regular position. He should string out the defensive perimeter by emulating a sweep, then drive upfield, leveling off for the goal line. The quarterback leads the play, picking up the first opponent who shows breaking across the line of scrimmage, or as soon as he turns upfield beyond our tackle's and end's double team block.

The frontside guard blocks the man over him and the center must cut off the middle linebacker. The center is taught to scramble on all fours, cutting off the linebacker. Both the backside guard and tackle cut off their defenders, and the backside end drives cross-field and blocks the farside secondary defender.

The ball carrier is taught to run with reckless power once he turns upfield. He must also use the proper lean for gaining yardage, as many defenders will be tackling the ball carrier from side angles. A powerful runner should be able to break tackles and run over pursuing defensive backs by dipping his shoulder after leveling off for the goal line.

The Off Tackle Power Play is set up by the power sweep. The power sweep cuts down or blocks the defensive end in, while the power off tackle drive keeps the defensive end honest by kicking the defender to the outside.

## Play-Action Passes

When we pass on the goal line, use the previously described sprint-out pass as well as the play-action pass. The offense likes to use the play-action pass because it tends to hold the defensive backs close to the line of scrimmage, looking for the anticipated run.

## Fullback Dive Pass

When running the Fullback Dive Pass, both of the ends block and the offense releases only one receiver. The lone receiver is the back in Diagram 3-24. The reason the frontside end blocks is that most secondary defenders key more heavily on the offensive end than on any other potential receiver. Therefore, the offensive end blocks aggressively to help draw the defensive secondary closer to the line of

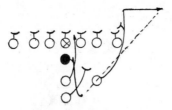

**Diagram 3-24**

scrimmage looking for the run. Meanwhile, the frontside offensive halfback fakes a block on the defensive end and slides off unnoticed into the flat for a quick pass from the quarterback.

This has proven to be a successful pass on first and second down plays, regardless of the yardage, as well as on a third down play. The quarterback should throw this flat pass on an angle so that if it is incomplete, the pass will be thrown out of bounds or beyond the defender's reach. To help create this angle and cut down the threat of a rushing lineman deflecting the pass, the frontside linemen are taught to block the defenders low. The low blocking technique by the frontside linemen helps to bring the defenders' hands down to protect or ward off the low fire-out blockers. This is especially important for the offensive end, because he is blocking the closest defender to the straight line between the quarterback and halfback. That is why the end must fire into this defender, taking away the defender's charge and blocking him low to keep his arms down to fight off the block.

The tailback is the offensive insurance blocker who is assigned the job of picking up the first defensive rusher who breaks through our offensive blocking protection. All of the offensive blockers are made aware of the fact that all goal line defenses are based upon their ability to penetrate by angling through the offensive line. Therefore, each day the blockers are taught to fire-out block, attacking various goal line defenses.

## Torpedo Pass

The Torpedo Pass is another play-action pass that is a good call near the goal line (Diagram 3-25). The offense selects this play-action pass because it runs the torpedo power play on the goal line. The right end is taught to catch the pass four to five yards downfield. The end runs for the seam or an opening in the opposition's secondary. The backside end runs his across pattern and has the option of hook-

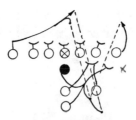

**Diagram 3-25**

ing over the middle, if the defender has a favorable lead cushion on our end, or continuing deeper behind the defensive secondary.

The quarterback must make a good fake to the tailback, then drop back three steps and be ready to throw quickly. Turning out on the defensive end is the tailback's assignment, and he should take the proper angle to drive the opponent to the outside, beyond the passer. All of the linemen are coached to use aggressive fire-out blocking resembling the torpedo running play.

## Power-I Counter Plays

If the opposition has an outstanding middle linebacker who is known for his pursuit, the offense likes to finesse him one way and come back with a counter play. Just as the linebacker begins to recover from the fake and begins to reverse his direction, the halfback is assigned to blast him from the opposite side. What the offense is actually doing to the point man is to isolate this defender with counter action, then block him from his blind side.

In Diagram 3-26, the tailback runs the Counter Play from the Power-I Formation, isolating the middle linebacker with our quarterback's fake to the fullback, who drives over the left offensive guard. The quarterback continues to reverse pivot and hands the ball off to

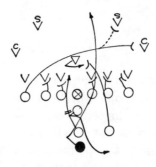

**Diagram 3-26**

the tailback. The tailback makes a quick stutter step to his left, then cuts off our right guard's outside hip. The check step helps to set up the timing between the hand-off and our halfback's block on the middle linebacker.

The right guard fires out on the defender over or inside of him; he is ready to unload on him because he is taught to expect the defender to penetrate, since this is a penetrating 65 Goal Line Defense. Usually the defender will be pinching to the inside on this short-yardage goal line situation. The right tackle takes his defender any way he wants to go, but the defender should be blocked outside whenever possible. The right end turns out on the defensive end, shielding the defensive end away from the play. The center engages the middle linebacker just prior to our halfback's torpedo block. The center should engage the middle linebacker because the defender may have a blitz called directly over the middle. Both the backside guard and tackle block their men inside or over them, and the backside end blocks shallow across field on the first secondary defender who shows.

The Counter-Action Play on the goal line is a good call, not only to isolate the middle linebacker, but also to cut down the pursuit of the 65 Goal Line Defense. Too often, goal line defenders go after the first potential ball carrier in an all-out effort, and cannot re-group against an offensive counter-action play.

## Power-I Scissors Pass

The three-part faking action by the bellying fullback's, scissoring halfback's, and rolling quarterback's paths helps to freeze the deep secondary defenders (Diagram 3-27). The bellying fullback is coached

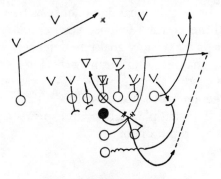

**Diagram 3-27**

to find an opening in the line and to start straight downfield. At approximately seven yards, the fullback is instructed to break off his downfield route, push off his inside foot, and make a break for the sidelines. The tight end is assigned to break straight downfield, then run his normal flag pass pattern. The reason the tight end is assigned to run a flag cut is to put the deep receiver in the same viewing angle of the passer as the fullback's flat pass pattern. The backside split end is instructed to run a drag pattern and find an opening crease in the deep defensive secondary. The quarterback is taught to reverse and fake a belly ride to the fullback, then make an inside fake hand-off with his backside hand. The quarterback then continues to roll outside and begins to turn upfield to attack the defensive corner. After the backside halfback blocks the defender responsible for containing the quarterback, the quarterback passes the ball to the fullback in the flat if the cornerback attacks the rolling out quarterback. If the cornerback drops back to defend against the pass, the quarterback is coached to yell, "run," and turn upfield.

All of the frontside linemen are instructed to use their normal, aggressive fire-out blocks. The backside offensive linemen are assigned to use the fan or drop-back pass protection blocks.

These are some of our basic goal line running plays and passes that the Power I practices each day in its practice sessions against the anticipated opposition's goal line defense. An occasional run or pass may be added against an opponent who uses a defense that may be susceptible to a particular offensive play off the Power-I formation.

The offense feels it must emphasize the goal line offense as much as the defense works on its goal line defenses. It is apparent that the offensive coaching staff must sell the entire offensive unit that it can score anytime it gets inside the opponent's ten yard line through the proper team execution. Team spirit and morale are just as important when moving the ball on the goal line offense as they are on the goal line defense. And the Power-I Offense is an excellent power offense to run through or pass over any goal line defense.

The following chapter describes how the Pro-I's offensive formation will make the reader a winner. The Pro-I's sweeps, options, isos, cuts, and misdirection plays are described. The explosive passing attack featuring drop-back, play-action, and sprint-out passes are also discussed in step-by-step fashion.

# 4

# THE PRO-I FORMATION

## How the Pro-I Offense Will Help You Win

The Pro-I offensive formation is a balanced run-pass attack that features three quick pass receivers plus two running threats in fine position to hit any hole along the line of scrimmage. When the Pro-I Formation was first adopted, there was a general feeling among many coaches that the I's backfield did not lend itself to a successful sweep play. The Southern California Power Sweep plus the I's Triple Option plays have disproved this theory.

This is an excellent attack for a coach who has one durable, option-running tailback that has the ability to make the intelligent quick cut for daylight. Since the formation spreads the defensive front, the running attack is assured of a consistent ground attack with adequate blocking up front.

The passing game is strengthened with three quick pass receivers who can go deep or find the open area against the stretched defensive secondary. This formation may utilize the sprint-out, drop-back, play-action, or a combination of these passes.

## The Advantages of the Pro-I Attack

1. The I-set has been perfectly designed for the sprint-out pass. The quarterback can easily sprint out in either direction and utilize either or both the fullback and the tailback as pass protectors.

2. The strongest feature of the I-set is that both the fullback and the tailback can attack any hole along the line of scrimmage.

3. The tailback is normally the better running back, and he can sweep or run off tackle in any direction.

4. When running the Triple Option, the tailback is always the pitchman in both directions.

5. The fullback may be utilized as a blocker or a faker; the amount of times the fullback carries the ball depends on his talent as a ball carrier.

6. The depth of the tailback (pitchman) on all option plays is advantageous, because it allows more separation between the quarterback and the pitchman. This makes it more difficult for one defender on the corner to play both the quarterback and the pitchman.

7. The alignment of the tailback is an advantage for all option plays, because it enables him to turn the corner more quickly from this I-alignment rather than the normal tailback's set position in the T-formation.

8. The depth of the tailback allows this running back a chance to get the ball deeper and to run for daylight, especially versus today's fast-pursuing defenses. This means a normal off tackle hole may well end up as a cut-back play, against the grain of the defensive pursuit, because a hole or seam opens up in the defensive front.

9. Discriminate offensive line blocking assignments plus the I-back's optional running techniques give the offense alternative points of attack along the line of scrimmage.

*Coaching Point*: Discriminate line blocking assigns the blocker to block his assigned defender in the direction the defender wants to go.

10. The two wide-outs help to widen the opposition's defense.

11. The continual deep threat of the three receivers, on or near the line of scrimmage, forces the defensive secondary to cover the deep threat of the bomb on all plays.

12. This offensive attack has the wide passing threat plus the strong inside running game.

## Requirements for the Pro I's Personnel

*Tailback*—The tailback must be an intelligent, durable runner. By "intelligent," we mean the tailback must be able to make the quick correct cut to daylight. He must be strong enough to be the main running back, and durable enough to run at full speed for the entire season. The tailback is a pure runner and is seldom required to block or catch passes.

*Fullback*—The fullback is selected for his blocking ability. He must be big enough to make the key lead, iso, or kick-out block. He should be the type of player who loves contact and will go out of his way to hit people. The fullback must be a team man, because he will not be a primary runner in the Pro-I attack.

*Quarterback*—The quarterback should be a passer, first, then a ball carrier. The quarterback should be chosen as a sprint-out passer, first, and a drop-back passer, second. He must be able to hit the sideline and the deep curl passes with consistency.

*Wide Receivers*—Pass receiving is the most important prerequisite for the wide receivers. These wide men must be able to catch the sideline and the curl passes. Both of these players must also learn how to make the successful run-off block.

*Tight End*—The tight end must have good size to be able to make the double team and the one-on-one blocks. He must also be able to run good pass routes and have good hands. Thus, he should have the blocking ability of an offensive tackle as well as the ability to make the clutch catch.

*Tackles*—The offensive tackle must be able to make the key one-on-one block. Using this formation and primarily discriminate blocking, the offensive tackle must be able to stay with his block and take the defender in the direction the defender wants to go. He must also be big enough to make the post block to set up the important double team block.

*Guards*—The guards must be able to block the defender on a one-on-one basis similar to the tackle's assignment. An important plus for the guard is that he must have the speed and quickness to make the trap and lead blocks on the sweeps. He does not have to be as big as the offensive tackle, but he must be strong enough to block the 44 defensive tackle.

*Center*—The center must be quick enough to block the middle guard one-on-one and to make the cut-off block. He must also be fast enough to pass block the outside defender when there is no down defender over him.

## The Pro-I Formation Alignment

The tailback lines up in a two-point stance with his heels six yards from the ball. The fullback lines up directly behind the quarterback, approximately four and one-half yards from the ball in a three-point stance. The tight end's split varies from one to three yards from the strongside offensive tackle. Both the wide-outs split out approximately ten yards from their closest teammates. This wide-out split depends on field position and how close the ball is placed from the nearside boundary (Diagram 4-1).

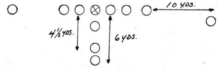

**Diagram 4-1**

## Pro I's Power Sweep

The critics against the I originally stated it was a poor formation for consistently turning the corner. The Power Sweep is a strong outside play featured by the Pro I. This Power Sweep can be run not only to the tight end's but also to the split end's side. The Power Sweep illustrated and described in the following pages is featured against various defenses and is run primarily to the formation's split end's side.

## Split Side Power Sweep

When running to the split end's side, the split end cracks back on the second widest defender to his side. This is the weakside safety-man in Diagram 4-2. Against the 53 Gap Stack Defense, the frontside tackle is assigned to block down on the #1 defender, and the frontside offensive guard uses his step-around blocking technique on the frontside #2 defensive linebacker (this is the same step-around block used versus the 44 Defense). The offensive center blocks back on the backside #2 man, and the backside tackle pulls and cuts off the #1 defender in the backside guard-tackle gap. The backside guard pulls and executes a lead block on the frontside cornerback. The fullback leads the split side sweep and overthrows on the #3 defender. The quarterback uses a reverse pivot (pivoting on his backside foot) and pitches to the tailback. The tailback must use a drop step to time the pitch, then run parallel to the line of scrimmage, following the backside guard's lead block. If the pulling guard kicks the cornerback out, the ball carrier cuts up inside of this guard's kick-out block. If the pulling guard is able to overthrow on the defensive cornerback, the ball carrier turns the corner around the guard's block.

Another sound method of blocking for the I's Power Sweep is to block down with the tight end and strong tackle, and pull both guards around the corner. The frontside guard is coached to pull and block the inside secondary defender, while the backside guard is assigned to lead the sweep and pick up the first defensive threat who shows. The fullback is assigned to cut down the #3 defender. The down-blocking assignment by the tight end has a tendency to force the defensive #3 man to close inside to stop the possible off tackle play (Diagram 4-3).

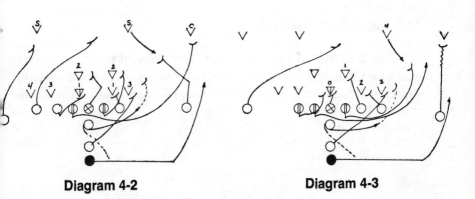

Diagram 4-2                                    Diagram 4-3

## Iso Versus 43 Defense

Against the slow-keying middle linebacker, the fullback goes straight at the middle linebacker and blasts this #0 defender head-on. The quarterback uses his reverse pivot and hands off to the tail-back, who follows his isoing fullback. The ball carrier is coached to favor the double team side of the center. Since the right offensive guard posts the left #1 defender, the center is assigned to drive into this defensive tackle, completing the double team block (Diagram 4-4).

If the middle linebacker is a fast keyer and quickly scallops to the point of the attack, the fullback blocks this #0 defender in the direction he wants to go. The tailback again follows the fullback and makes his break off the lead back's iso block. The left tackle blocks the #1 defender man-on-man, and the frontside offensive tackle turns out on the #2 defender (Diagram 4-5).

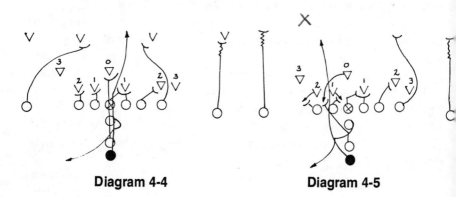

**Diagram 4-4**                          **Diagram 4-5**

## The Tight End Around

For a change of pace, the Tight End Around play may develop into a long gainer if executed properly off a successful isolation game. The quarterback must make a good, long fake to the tailback and hand

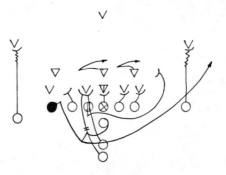

**Diagram 4-6**

the ball off to the tight end at four and one-half yards depth. The tight end takes one step forward with his inside foot and sets a course for the tail of the fullback's original alignment. The quarterback is responsible for placing the ball (with his left hand) into the tight end's pocket. Once the end receives the ball, he is instructed to follow the left guard's pulling lead block. This play is particularly effective against the fast-shuffling defensive linebackers, as illustrated in Diagram 4-6.

## Pro-I Offense Versus the #3 Defender

When attacking a defense, we like to select a particular defender and attack the area he neglects. The "area he neglects" means if a particular defender moves outside to stop our quick pitch, we run inside; if he stays at home to protect his inside area, we utilize the quick pitch and go around this particular defender.

Using the Pro-I Formation, we designate the #3 defensive man to the split end's side as the defender whom we wish to attack. First, the quarterback wants to make this defender outside conscious, so we feature the quick pitch against the #3 man (defensive end) versus the Monster 52 Defense. Diagram 4-7 features the quick ride to the fullback to hold the #3 defender, and the quick pitch to the I-back, who begins in motion. Once the quarterback realizes that the #3 man does not intend to cover or loosen to defend against the tailback's motion, the quarterback fakes to the fullback, pulls the ball out of the fullback's pocket, and pitches the ball out quickly to the tailback. The fullback is assigned to block the defender whichever way the #3 man goes. If he stays (Diagram 4-7), the fullback uses his over-throw block on the #3 man.

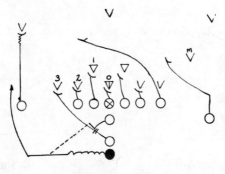

**Diagram 4-7**

If the #3 defender honors the motion and begins to loosen or feather to the outside, the quarterback makes a quick fake to the fullback, pulls the ball out of the dive back's pocket, and turns up inside of the fullback's kick-out block (Diagram 4-8). On both plays, the split end sprints straight downfield and runs off the deep outside secondary defender, then comes under control to block the deep defender. Normally, the deep pass defender shuffles quickly backward, honoring the apparent deep cut of the split end, then pulls up and begins to come back to defend against the apparent run. The split end is then coached to slow block the deep back, blocking the defender in any direction he wants to go. Thus, the split end stalks the deep back and blocks him at the last moment (Diagram 4-8).

Using this same play sequence, the quarterback may also want to pass the ball, particularly to take advantage of the quick-rotating defensive secondary, who often try to move their deep middle safety over to compensate for the tailback's motion. The Monster back is also rotated to inherit the deep middle one-third defensive pass zone as soon as the deep safety begins his assigned move. When this happens, the quarterback has the option of passing the ball off to the tailback, who may flare down the sidelines for the deep pass. The passer may also throw back to the tight end, who attempts to beat the Monster defender up the middle for the bomb. The split end is the third choice as he runs a straight route, gathers himself as if to block on the Quick Pitch (Diagram 4-7) or the Quarterback Keeper (Diagram 4-8), then flashes by the deep outside defender on a deep post cut. Again, the fullback blocks the #3 defender regardless of the #3 man's assignment (Diagram 4-9).

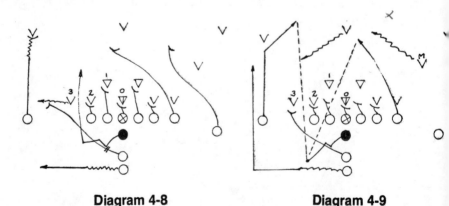

**Diagram 4-8**                                      **Diagram 4-9**

## Pro I's Adjusted I-Slot Formation

Diagram 4-10 illustrates the Pro I's adjusted I-Slot Formation. The I-Slot is nothing more than a "Pro Look," only now the flanker back has moved into a slotback's position to the split end's side. The end away from the slotback may be tight or in a split alignment. This adjustment gives this offense a four-back running threat.

## The Advantages of the I-Slot Attack

1. Forces the defensive secondary to show its secondary coverage immediately.
2. Stretches the defensive secondary across the width of the field.
3. Forces the defensive secondary to defend in depth versus the continual threat of the bomb.
4. Gives the attack three quick pass receivers.
5. Gives the running attack interior power, featuring the isolation plays and a strong off tackle play.
6. The close slotback gives this offense a four-back running threat.
7. The slotback is an all-purpose back lined up one yard behind the normal tight end's position in the I-Slot Formation.
8. The tailback or the slotback has the ability to run in motion in either direction.
9. Short motion by the slotback may overshift or balance up this formation.
10. This formation has the best of both worlds, because it has two wide-outs plus a four-back running threat.

## The I-Blast

The I-Blast (Diagram 4-10) is normally run directly at the linebacker. This is an isolation play where the offensive blockers isolate the defensive linebacker by blocking all other defenders away from him. The fullback is the assigned blast blocker—he runs directly at the isolated defender and blocks the linebacker in any direction the linebacker moves. If the linebacker decides not to move, the blocker

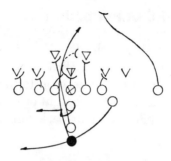

**Diagram 4-10**

runs right over this defender and cuts him down. A maximum split by both the frontside guard and tackle normally helps to isolate the inside linebacker. These splits also help to give the blockers better blocking angles on their assigned defenders.

The quarterback uses a reverse pivot and steps backward to hand the ball off to the ball carrier, deep enough to give him a chance to make his cut to daylight. The timing of the reverse pivot allows the ball carrier to cut right off the tail of the blasting fullback.

Diagram 4-11 points out how the I-Blast isolates and attacks the inside 44 linebacker. The blast versus the 44 Defense often becomes more of a cut-back play, since the backside inside 44 linebacker often overpursues or scallops into the potential hole. If the backside linebacker scrapes toward the apparent off tackle hole, the blast may turn into a double team block (Diagram 4-12).

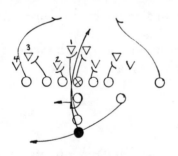

**Diagram 4-11**

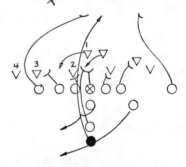

**Diagram 4-12**

When attacking the 61 Defense, the ball carrier must realize that the middle linebacker will be the point of the offensive attack. Diagram 4-13 shows the blast by the fullback on the #0 middle linebacker, who is also blocked from the blind side by the right offensive tackle. This double team helps to open up the middle for the tailback's thrust. All of the other offensive linemen have excellent blocking angles on their respective assigned defenders.

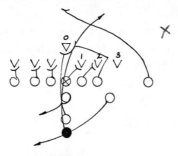

**Diagram 4-13**

## The Cut (Sprint-Out Draw) Play

The Cut Play is one of the finest plays in football. It features a quick outside threat with the beginning outside path of the tailback. The quarterback's path looks like a quick sprint-out path. A power block by the offensive frontside tackle and slotback helps to open the off tackle hole. The kick-out block by the fullback (on the first defender outside of the double team block) and the backside guard's pulling seal block have helped to spring many running backs away for long gainers (Diagram 4-14).

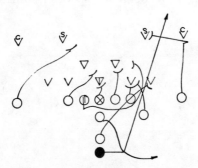

**Diagram 4-14**

## I Counter Option

The Counter Play off the I is a misdirection maneuver that helps to set up the offensive linemen's blocking. The countering fullback's route and the quarterback's reverse pivot help to freeze the middle linebacker (#0 man) long enough to let the offensive center execute a smooth cut-off block on him. Double teaming the defensive #1 man forces the two defenders to shuffle down the line of scrimmage and attack the quarterback. Thus, the #2 defender dictates the offensive pitch-out, and the slotback and frontside split end use their run-off blocking techniques to eliminate the #3 and #4 men (Diagram 4-15).

## Misdirect Power Block

When running from an I-Wing formation, the defense often keys the fullback because he normally takes the defense to the ball. Other defenses key the "I"—this means they key both the I-backs (fullback and tailback) in order to get to the ball. In either case, the misdirected offensive running play is a successful key-breaker. Diagram 4-16 shows both the fullback and the tailback starting in one direction, and at the last moment, the tailback cuts back to the opposite side of the formation. To make sure the blockers at the point of the attack get their perfect blocking angles, the play calls for the split end to drive block to his inside and help the frontside offensive tackle power block the defensive #2 man. This also gives the frontside split end a fine blocking angle on the frontside #3 defender. The slotback fakes an inside step and allows the split end to cross his face. Then the slotback turns out on the #3 defender. All of the offensive interior and perimeter blockers' blocks have been set up by the misdirected backfield's maneuvering.

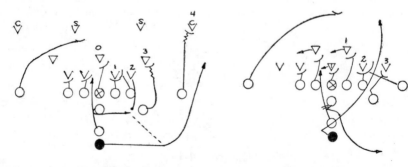

**Diagram 4-15**                              **Diagram 4-16**

## Play-Action Passing Success

The continual success of the play-action pass depends on the execution of the play-action fake, the aggressive fire-out line blocking techniques, the receiver running his correct route, and the passer's ability to complete the pass. The most important phase of play-action passing is the aggressive fire-out blocking by the offensive blockers. This explosive one-on-one blocking technique minimizes the defensive linebackers' and secondary's defensive pass keys. These aggressive fire-out blocking techniques, combined with a well-timed running fake, make the play-action pass a most explosive feature of the total passing attack.

## The I-Slot Counter Bootleg Pass

The I-Slot is an excellent formation from which to run the Counter Bootleg Pass, both to the overloaded slot side and to the tight end's side. On both of these plays, the fullback usually slips out of his I-alignment and surprises the defense by sneaking out into the flat area unmolested. Whenever the fullback makes the catch with the counter action off the backfield fakes, he usually turns upfield for a fine chance to make a long gainer against a defensive secondary that has run out of position, and with deep receivers who are in good positions to pull back and block after the short counter pass completion.

## Counter Bootleg Pass away from the Slot

The Counter Bootleg Pass away from the Slot is a consistent call versus the three deep, locked-in pass defense. The key block is made by the left offensive tackle, who fires out aggressively into the defensive tackle and invites him to take an inside course, since the defender is influenced by the tailback's counter fake. If the defensive tackle does not take the inside course, the offensive left tackle is coached to reach block on the defender's outside leg. The offensive left guard and center fire out aggressively to cut off both of their defenders, using their scramble reach blocking techniques. The right guard pulls, gains depth, and sets up in a position to block the defensive right end (Diagram 4-17).

The pulling guard may use one of three techniques: First, if the wide defender (#3 man) drops off the line to cover the flat, the offensive pulling guard signals "run" to the quarterback and escorts the field general downfield (Diagram 4-18). Second, when the defen-

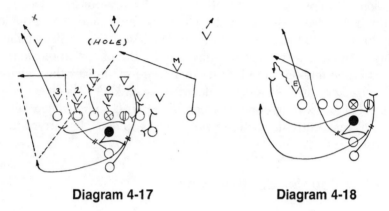

**Diagram 4-17**                    **Diagram 4-18**

sive #3 man hangs on the line of scrimmage, the pulling guard goes after the #3 defender, attacking his outside leg. The passer now hits the fullback in the flat, or he may wish to tuck the ball away and run with it. In this case, the fullback is taught to turn upfield and lead the running quarterback (Diagram 4-19). Third, if the defensive #3 man attempts to use his contain rush and attacks from an outside-in angle, the pulling guard is coached to turn out on the containing #3 man and block the defender to the outside. Now the bootlegging quarterback merely rolls out, steps up inside of the pulling guard's kick-out block, and delivers his strike to the fullback open in the flat (Diagram 4-20).

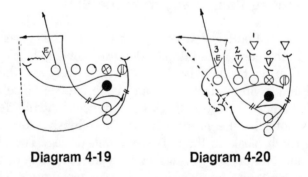

**Diagram 4-19**                    **Diagram 4-20**

Both the backside offensive tackle and slotback step up with the inside foot and turn out on their respective backside defenders. The tight end is coached to run a deep arrow cut right through the deep secondary defender who is assigned to cover the deep outside one-third zone. The split end is assigned to run a quick, shallow drag pass pattern, looking for an opening over the middle in the "hole" (Diagram 4-17).

The fullback takes off and runs a flat pass route, sliding out into the clear between the tight end's and the offensive left tackle's original positions.

The quarterback opens up or makes a quick flash fake to the fullback, then reverses to ride the tailback with a long ride to the backside. Then the quarterback hides the ball and slowly turns to begin his bootleg pass route, rolling out toward the tight end's side. The option to continue to roll to the outside, to pull up and deliver the pass, or to tuck the ball away and run is predicated upon the block of the pulling backside offensive guard, as illustrated in Diagrams 4-18, 4-19, and 4-20.

## Counter Bootleg Pass to the Slot

The Counter Bootleg Pass is actually a run-pass option by the quarterback. He is coached to key the Monster man: if the Monster takes the deep flat pass pattern, run by the slotback. The quarterback has the option of passing to the fullback running the short flat route or of faking the pass and running with the ball (Diagram 4-21).

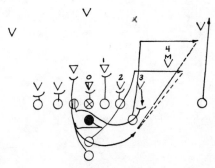

**Diagram 4-21**

All of the blocking assignments are similar to the Counter Bootleg Pass Away from the Slot that was shown in Diagram 4-17, except the bootleg to the slot side is a flood pass pattern of three receivers: the wide end running his deep arrow route, the deep flat route of the slotback, and the short flat pattern by the fullback.

The quarterback's first thought is to "try to get outside of the defensive containment." Then the quarterback has a multi-optional selection. If the #3 defender contains the passer and forces him to pull up, the passer is coached to key the Monster. No matter who the Monster covers, he will be wrong, as the passer hits the open, outnumbered pass receiver.

## The Crack Pass

A passing sequence off the split side power sweep is the Crack Pass. The blocking along the line of scrimmage is similar to that of the Power Sweep. Only now, the split end fakes his crack-back block on the weakside safety and continues inside to catch the pass between the seam of the strongside safetyman and the weakside cornerback. This seam is widened by the weakside safetyman moving up toward the line of scrimmage on his invert route to his assigned weakside flat zone.

The quarterback uses his reverse pivot, fakes the Power Sweep pitch-out, and sprints back, pulling up behind his right tackle. The passer looks for the split end on his crack pass route, first; if he is not open, the passer throws a fly pass to the streaking tight end, who is streaking deep in the opposite seam (Diagram 4-22).

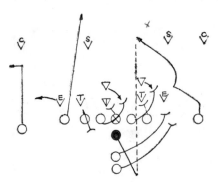

**Diagram 4-22**

## Flare Pass Versus 52 Monster Defense

When the quarterback attacks the 52 Monster Defense, quick tailback motion off the I can quickly balance the offensive passing attack. If the defensive secondary does not immediately rotate into a four deep man-to-man defense, the pass defense is in trouble. Diagram 4-23 illustrates the I-back running a short-motion flare route opposite the Monster. The split end holds the deep one-third pass defender deep with his post cut, and the I-back is free in the quick flat, running with a head of steam as he catches the ball. The fullback blocks the first defender outside of the tackle's block. The quarterback is instructed to pull up and set up just behind his offensive tackle's original position. The passer must be ready for a quick release to hit the flaring tailback as the receiver begins to turn upfield.

## Flanker's Quick Drag
## Versus Man to Man (Four Deep)

Against the four deep, man-to-man pass defense, the I-back attempts to draw the weak safetyman out of position by influencing him with motion. The tight end runs a quick hook pass pattern to hold the strong safetyman, while the flankerback pushes off straight downfield for three steps, then makes a quick drag cut across the middle to catch the ball in the open area vacated by the weak safety's motion assignment. The quarterback begins to sprint out to the strong side, then pulls up behind his strongside offensive guard. The passer looks directly at the hooking tight end, then hits the free flanker in the open zone (Diagram 4-24).

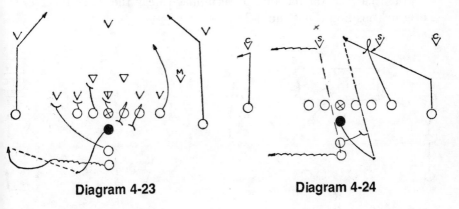

Diagram 4-23          Diagram 4-24

## I Wide Slot

Against the two deep, five underneath zone pass coverage, the offense should split both of the ends as wide as possible. The width of the wide receivers helps to spread out the two deep safetymen so the slot man can get open in the crease between these two deep defenders. The two wide offensive ends run their deep fly cuts to help pull the deep defenders wide to cover the deep fly pass pattern.

A straight drop-back pocket pass is used by the quarterback, and he is coached to look off and make a quick passing fake to one of the wide receivers. The fake helps the timing of the pass and helps to draw one of the safeties away from the deep middle zone. The slot receiver times his up pass pattern to split the crease between the two deep safeties (Diagram 4-25).

## I-Slot Read Pass
## Versus Five Underneath Coverage

The quarterback is taught to attack the width of the five underneath, two deep zone pass defense. The Read Pass features the wide receiver running a deep fly cut, trying to beat the deep safetyman to his side. The second inside receiver (slotback) runs a deep sideline pass pattern, about eighteen yards deep. This depth takes the slotback into a pocket between the deep safety's one-half keep zone and the left defensive cornerback's flat zone pass defense assignments. The third pass receiver is the fullback, who is assigned to set block to his right, then swing wide into a position where he is taught to receive a potential pass on the line of scrimmage near the wide receiver's original position (Diagram 4-26).

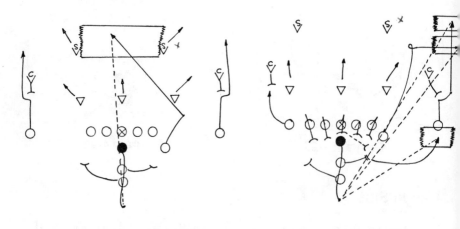

**Diagram 4-25**                                    **Diagram 4-26**

## Stop Pass Versus the Two Deep Secondary

Since the widest areas are the most open zones of the two deep secondary, the Stop Pass pattern is an excellent call. The two offensive wide-outs in their deep stop-pass patterns help to pull the two deep safetyman out wide and deep to defend against these wide deep patterns. The tight end then runs a post into the open middle zone.

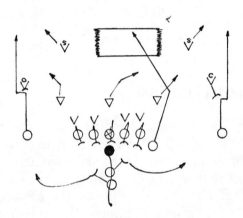

**Diagram 4-27**

The tight end must run his pass pattern under control, and may have to slow down in the open area (Diagram 4-27).

## The One-Man Pass Pattern

The passer needs maximum protection at all times. This means the offense may be forced to keep the tight end and the two backs in blocking protection, and can only send out the wide receiver to that side.

The quarterback sprints out to the strong side with both I-backs leading the sprint-out. The passer has a pass-run option, and is coached to run whenever he can make five or more yards or the first down on a third-and-long situation. The tight end also is assigned to block. The wide receiver has a three-option pass pattern. He may run (1) a sideline and up, (2) a hitch or hook, or (3) a deep post pattern (Diagram 4-28).

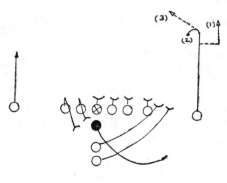

**Diagram 4-28**

## Tailback Motion Flare Pass

The quarterback sprints out and tries to hit the tailback in the circled area just as the tailback reaches the line of scrimmage (Diagram 4-29). If the passer cannot hit the motioned receiver in this area, he is coached not to throw the ball in the receiver's waved-line area. The reason this flat area is taboo is that the Monster defender is assigned to cover the flat area. Whenever the passer is not able to hit the flaring tailback in the circled area, he tries to hit the split end on a short post route. The area in which to deliver the pass to the posting split receiver is directly over the Monster's original position. The slotback is coached to run a tight hook cut to stop the inside frontside 52 linebacker from intercepting the short push pass.

The fullback is assigned to block the #3 defender, and the passer is encouraged to challenge the corner before releasing the ball. Whenever the passer can gain five yards or more, he is encouraged to run.

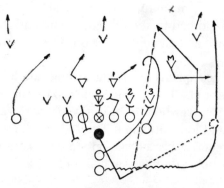

**Diagram 4-29**

## Bootleg Drag Flag Pass

A good change-up from the normal Tailback Motion Pass is the Bootleg Drag Flag Pass (Diagram 4-20). All of the pass routes and backfield action start out similar to the normal sprint-out passes. After the passer sprints back five steps, he starts to roll back toward the weak side of the formation. The split end is assigned to begin a regular drag route, but to break off into a flag cut just as he reaches a point opposite the offensive tackle's original position. This pass cut, along with the apparent sprint-out pass action by the quarterback, often lulls the weakside cornerback to sleep. As soon as the deep defender sees the apparent bootleg action by the quarterback, it is often too late for the deep defender to cover the split end's flag cut.

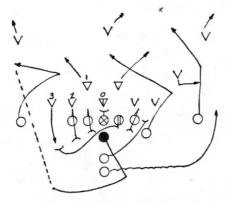

**Diagram 4-30**

The left guard set steps and pulls deep toward the weakside to pass protect against the #3 defender. If the flag man is not open, the passer is instructed to look for the slotback dragging over the middle.

## Triple Shot Post Pass

Against the Sky safety force or invert defense to the split end's side versus the Triple Option attack, the Quick Post Pass takes advantage of this secondary stunt (Diagram 4-31). The quarterback fakes the dive to the dive back, and the frontside guard pulls and blocks the first defender who shows outside of the offensive tackle's block. As soon as the quarterback takes his first step, he checks the inside safety's path. If he takes an inverted sky course, the quarterback is

coached to take one step back and drop the ball to the split end in the
crease between the outside cornerback and the backside defensive
safetyman.

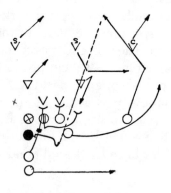

**Diagram 4-31**

# 5

## THE DOUBLE WIDE SLOT OFFENSE

### How Will the Double Wide Slot Offense Help You?

The Double Wide Slot Offense features an attack that has the striking potential of scoring on any given play from any position on the gridiron. This offense demonstrates a balanced run or pass program that takes advantage of any open area the defense presents. If the defense uses an unbalanced, overshifted, or Monster defense, the Double Wide Slot can attack it with an assorted number of audibles, counter options, reverses, and throwback passes to the weakside. This attack forces the defense to use a balanced alignment.

Pass plays on any down are normal occurrences with four quick pass receivers on or near the line of scrimmage. All types of motions and shifts emphasize the big play in this offense. The four potential pass receivers' deep routes run off the deep secondary defenders; it is an easier method to run off these defenders than it is to block them on basic running plays. The quarterback's sprint-out pass-run action,

plus the bootleg maneuvers, places added pressure on the corner
defenders (Diagram 5-1).

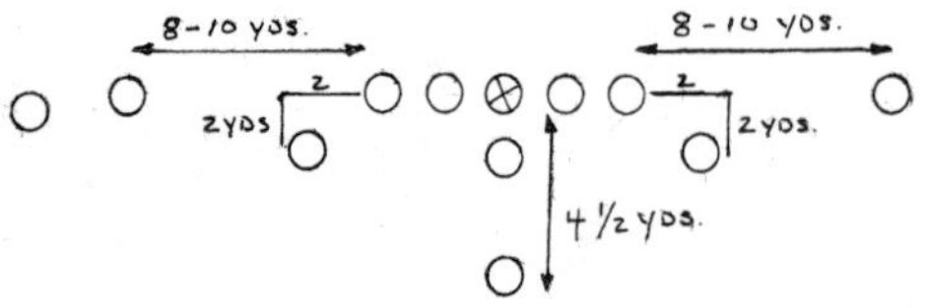

**Diagram 5-1**

## The Advantages of
## The Double Wide Slot Attack

1. This is a balanced formation that features the run and the pass
equally.

2. All of the runs and passes are designed to go all the way.

3. The four quick potential receivers, on or near the line of
scrimmage, normally force the four deep, man-to-man alignment.

4. This formation lends itself to a variation of offensive motion,
counter plays, and play-action passes.

5. The width of the double slot alignment often eliminates double coverage of the potential pass receivers.

6. The secondary must defend in depth, because of the alignment of the potential quick four receivers to run deep pass patterns.

7. The formation also spreads the defensive perimeter so wide
that it cuts down on the effectiveness of the opposition's gang-tackling
techniques.

8. Against the four deep secondary alignment, the offense normally emphasizes the running attack.

9. The attack emphasizes a passing game versus a three deep
secondary alignment, because this secondary allows more open areas
for the four quick receivers.

10. The two wide ends eliminate at least one defensive man to
each side merely by releasing downfield as potential receivers. It is
easier to teach the wide men to run a pass pattern than to block.

11. Motion and counter plays minimize pursuit and the defensive team's gang-tackling techniques.

12. Many of the receivers' pass patterns are predicated upon the
position and alignment of the deep defender rather than on being
called previously in the huddle.

13. This attack forces each opponent to adopt a new defense against this wide-open attack.

14. This spread formation forces the defense to retreat from their normal nine man front.

15. This formation lends itself to passing on any down or in any given field position.

16. The linemen always execute a fire-out blocking technique on runs or passes, which eliminates a pass "key" for any pass defenders.

17. It is practically impossible to double cover both split ends, because that would leave only seven defenders to cover the other nine offensive players.

18. The Double Wide Slot forces the opposition to balance their defense. If the defense overshifts with motion, the quarterback is coached to run counters, bootlegs, and throw-back passes to the weak side (fewest defenders).

## Requirements for
## The Double Wide Slot Personnel

The personnel requirements for the Double Wide Slot Offense are:

*Quarterback*—The field general should be a good sprint-out and play-action passer. He must work at passing on the run and have the running ability to turn the corner on pass-run options.

*Fullback*—He should be a strong, quick runner who is a hard-nosed offensive performer. This performer must be big enough to block the contain man on sweeps and to knock down potential pass rushers. Quickness may be substituted for size. The fullback must have strong legs and must demonstrate sound faking ability.

*Slotbacks*—Must have speed rather than size. Both of these performers must be able to make the drive block, with the tackle as the post blocker. They must be good pass receivers and have better than average running ability to make the sweep a consistent offensive weapon.

*Split Ends*—The split ends must have the dual ability to make the big catch and to make the run-off block on the deep secondary defenders. Since the ends are always split, size is not a prerequisite for the flank positions.

*Interior Five Offensive Linemen*—The interior blockers must have the ability to scramble block for the sprint-out and play action passes, as well as the sweeps and off tackle plays. The interior line-men in the Double Wide Slot should have good size; however, quick-ness is more important than power.

## The Basic Double Wide Slot Drive Series

With short motion by one of the slotbacks, most plays may be run from the Double Wide Slot Formation. The inside Drive Series has been very successful in the past, especially with a smart, strong-running fullback. By "smart," we mean a fullback who is intelligent enough to be an option runner.

*Fullback Give*

This option runner (fullback) is taught to cut directly over the frontside offensive guard and to cut for daylight, depending on the guard's block. This means that if the guard blocks the #1 defender to the outside, the ball carrier is taught to cut to his inside, and vice-versa. When the blocker takes the defender straight backward, the fullback is coached to get as many yards as possible. Thus, the frontside guard is referred to as a discriminate blocker, who is coached to block the #1 defender to whichever side the defender chooses to go. The words "option running" refer to the ball carrier who is given the assignment to cut for daylight, depending on the guard's block at the point of attack (Diagram 5-2).

Diagram 5-2 illustrates the fullback breaking inside as the right guard turns out on the #1 man (defensive inside 52 Oklahoma linebacker). The blocking along the line of scrimmage is one-on-one as the ball carrier has option running to cut the play to the backside. This is why our backside offensive tackle hooks the backside #2 de-fender, because the ball carrier has the option of breaking the play in the backside tackle's area to cut against the grain of the defensive team's pursuit pattern. The fullback's option routes are shown in Diagram 5-3. This is why we teach the quarterback to reach back to give the ball to the fullback, so the ball carrier has plenty of room to run his backside cut. The quarterback puts the left slotback in short motion, so the slot man will be in the offensive set position (behind the offensive backside tackle) once the ball has been snapped. The left slot-back now runs his normal inside drive course, cutting right off the hip of the diving fullback. Immediately after the quarterback has handed the ball off to the fullback, he is taught to fake to the slotback

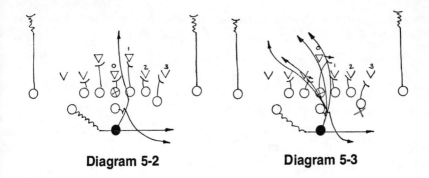

Diagram 5-2                            Diagram 5-3

as the second part of the drive play. After faking to these two backs, the quarterback continues to roll to his right as if he had the ball and was continuing to sweep the right end, rolling to his right for a possible pass.

Naturally, the more successful the fullback is with his dive play, the more successful the other facets of the Drive Series will be.

### The Halfback Drive

The give to the second man off the drive is blocked exactly as the give to the first man (fullback). Against the 53 Defense, the center blocks #0, the frontside guard blocks #1, the frontside tackle blocks down on #2, the right slotback turns out on the #3 defender, and the backside blockers block their normal #2 and #3 assignments. We do not like to send our backside blockers crossfield for three reasons. First, we want to protect the slot man's motion route against a possible blitz or fire angle stunt from the backside, especially when the slotback starts in motion. Second, the defensive deep secondary cannot read a run from our backside crossfield route. Third, as stated previously, we like to block the backside defenders one-on-one to encourage the cut-back play by the Drive Series' ball carriers.

The quarterback makes a quick fake to the diving fullback, then slips the ball off to the second man through. The ball carrier cuts off the frontside tackle's block. In Diagram 5-4 versus the 53 Defense, the defensive tackle (#2) lines up inside of our frontside offensive tackle; so the frontside tackle merely blocks down to cut off the #2 defender. The right slotback turns out on the #3 man, and the ball carrier has clear sailing. If the defensive tackle was head-up on the frontside offensive tackle, the offensive tackle would block him any way he wanted to go. The ball carrier would then use his option running assignment and make the most advantageous cut possible (Diagram 5-4).

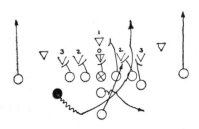

**Diagram 5-4**

### The Quarterback Counter

One counter play that has been a consistent gainer off the Drive Series is the Quarterback Counter. This play works best against the fast-flowing 52 linebackers, who begin to overpursue the Drive Series. To keep these 52 Oklahoma linebackers honest, the quarterback reaches backward a little deeper to the first offensive back (fullback); after a slight delay to study the backside 52 linebacker, the quarterback sets off to run an option course behind the one-on-one blocking of the left side of the offensive line. Once the quarterback reaches the line of scrimmage, he should run like a fullback—keep both hands on the ball, run low, and dip the inside shoulder. Diagram 5-5 illustrates the quarterback running at the point of the attack between the #1 and #2 defenders. Against the hanging 52 linebackers, the Quarterback Counter would normally be run between the linebacker (#1) and the defensive middle guard (#0).

### The Quarterback Run-Pass Play

The fourth play in this series is the Quarterback Run-Pass Option play. On this play call, the quarterback fakes to the dive back and the second man through (left slot-back) and rolls out, hiding the ball on his right hip. As the quarterback moves, he is taught to key the #4 defender. If the secondary is in a four deep defense, the #4 defender may come up from his inside safety position to contain the quarterback. The rolling quarterback drops off the pass over his head to the left slotback, who has slid out into the flat. If the right split end is open on a post cut, the passer will of course hit this streaking wide receiver for a long bomb (Diagram 5-6).

If the #4 inside safetyman attempts to run an invert course

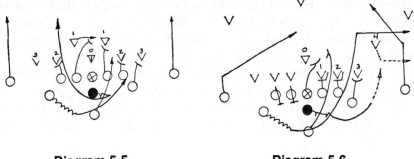

Diagram 5-5                                    Diagram 5-6

(dotted line in Diagram 5-6), the quarterback fakes the pass, tucks the ball away, and sprints downfield.

The right wide receiver (split end) is coached to run a flag route whenever the widest secondary defender attempts to roll up to contain the quarterback and the #4 inside safetyman tries to take the deep outside one-third zone. This is an easy read for the split end—as he starts downfield, he sees the outside defender attacking to contain and the inside safety attempting to cover the deep outside one-third zone. The flag cut by the wide receiver is run away from this defender and is an almost impossible area to cover (Diagram 5-7). Again, if the right split end is not open right at this point, the passer simply drops off the pass to the open receiver in the flat.

If the opposition tries to run a Monster 52 Defense to the right side, we would simply call an automatic to run the play to the opposite side, away from the Monster Man (Diagram 5-8). As the reader can see in the diagram, we have the defense outnumbered with a free man in the flat. If the three deep secondary attempts to roll, we run the same play; but, again, the wide receiver runs a flag cut away from the roll and makes the middle safetyman cover the deep outside

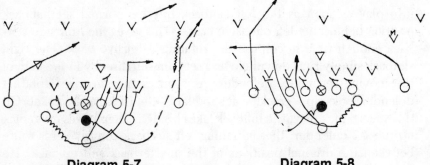

Diagram 5-7                                    Diagram 5-8

one-third zone. This is a very difficult task for even the fastest of safety defenders (Diagram 5-9). Again, if the flag route is not open for some unforeseeable reason, the quarterback drops off the pass to the second man through, in the flat area (Diagram 5-9).

This is why the Monster Overshift Defense, or any overshifted defense, is not successful versus the Double Wide Slot Offense. If the defense remains in their three deep pass defense and does not attack the quarterback, the quarterback merely tucks the ball away and runs.

## The Pick Pass

Some defensive secondaries attempt to run the Monster or Rover defender across the formation to follow the offensive man in motion. When this happens, the quarterback is coached to use a simple basketball pick play to stop this defender. Diagram 5-10 features this pick-off maneuver by the frontside slot-back. The quarterback is coached to run short motion and time the snap so the ball can be put

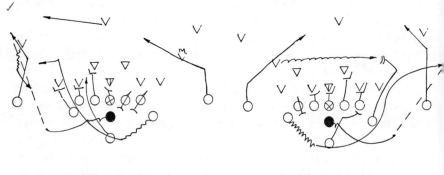

Diagram 5-9                          Diagram 5-10

into play as soon as the left slotback hits his normal set halfback position behind the left offensive tackle. This gives the frontside slotback enough time to confuse the rotating defensive back. The right slotback simply runs downfield and sets himself directly in the path of the moving secondary defender. As soon as the surprised rotating defender looks up, "crack!"—it's too late—the pick has been set. On this special pick play, the fullback fakes his dive, then levels off to pick up the #3 defender; the motioning left slotback continues his route between the original positions of the quarterback and fullback. He then runs his flat course and becomes free as a result of his teammate's slotback pick play.

## The Sprint Pass

Some defensive teams line up with a four-man rush and try to put an outside linebacker outside of each slotback to take away the flat. The Split-Forty Defense, as pictured in Diagram 5-11, attempts to accomplish this defensive perimeter coverage. When this happens, the Sprint-Out Pass is called, and the left wide receiver, left slotback, and fullback run a team flood pattern. All three of these receivers run a flood pass pattern, with a flag cut by the wide receiver, an arrow type cut by the slotback, and a flat route by the fullback. Usually the fullback is open. Often the slot-back is faster than most outside linebackers, and he, too, is often open. A fourth key receiver is the backside slotback, who runs a backside drag pass pattern into the open middle of the flowing three deep secondary defense (Diagram 5-11). The quarterback has a final option—of turning upfield and scrambling for as many yards as he can possibly gain.

## The Fullback Trap

The Double Wide Slot Fullback Trap is an excellent play on third down and long yardage. Many defenses attempt to defend the Double Wide Slot attack with a Pro-type Sixty-One Defense and a four-across-the-board secondary. This defensive alignment is particularly used on the third down and long situations. Therefore, the Quick Fullback Trap often develops into a long gainer for the offense on a third-and-long, or on any given down and distance (Diagram 5-12).

The left guard is the key trap man—his assignment is to trap the first defender who shows beyond the center. Normally, this is the frontside or playside defensive #1 man. The center blocks back on the backside #1 defender, and the right offensive tackle blocks down on the middle linebacker. On the long-yardage play, the middle

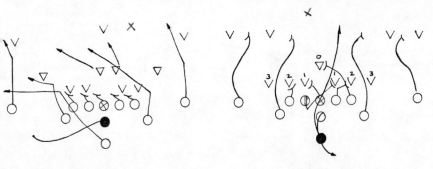

**Diagram 5-11**                    **Diagram 5-12**

linebacker usually begins to drop back to play the pass as the quarterback begins to retreat from the center. Then the linebacker realizes that the fullback has been slipped the ball and is running a zero trap. At the last moment, as the middle #0 linebacker gathers himself for an all-out, head-on attack versus the approaching fullback, the right offensive tackle hits him from the blind frontside with a smashing, head-on shoulder block. But the most strategic block is assigned to the frontside right offensive guard. He is coached to set up on the frontside #1 defender and influence him for the trap block of the left trapping guard. The right guard then turns out on the frontside #2 defender after he sets up the #1 defender for the trap. A quick open step backward gives the advancing fullback room to clear the quarterback and make his cut off the trapping guard's block. Once the ball carrier reaches the line of scrimmage, he is taught to look for the down block on the linebacker by the offensive right tackle and to cut off his block. The two outside potential receivers to each side are taught to take an inside-out angle and block the deep secondary defenders over them.

Many five man line defensive teams adjust their alignment to an Eagle look to help the linebackers defend against the two quick receivers to each side of the Double Wide Slot Formation. Whenever the quarterback sees this defensive alignment, he is normally urged to call an automatic for a fullback quick trap play. The center posts the #0 defender, and the frontside guard drives down on him. The frontside offensive tackle sets an influence block toward the defensive #1 man, then turns out and blocks the #2 linebacker. The backside guard is assigned to trap the influenced #1 defender. Both the backside tackle and slotback seal off their respective defenders to prevent defensive pursuit from overtaking the quick-hitting fullback. The right slot-back uses a turn-out block to screen the #3 defender away from the point of the attack (Diagram 5-13).

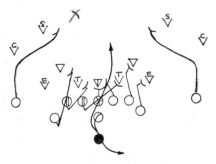

**Diagram 5-13**

The quarterback is taught to open up toward the fullback and step back in his direction. The reason the quarterback is coached to step back toward the fullback is to give him the ball soon enough so he can make his quick cut off the trapping guard's block. The quarterback is instructed to pull back his left foot so he does not force the ball carrier (fullback) too wide, away from the point of attack. The ball carrier must hit as quickly as possible and set his path directly off the butt of the pulling guard. He should favor or run as close to the double team block as possible. Against the two deep safety alignment, as illustrated in Diagram 5-13, we want the ball carrier to sprint straight upfield, try to split the safeties in half, and go for the score.

## The Slot Counter Trap

The Slot Counter Trap Play is a favorite of the Double Wide Slot Formation versus the Split-Forty Defense, because the counter trap is executed by the backside offensive tackle. The advantage of the tackle making the trap is that the backside (left) guard, center and frontside (right) guard all have excellent angles on their assigned defenders (Diagram 5-14).

Since the defensive tackles are lined up on the outside shoulder of the guards, the backside guard's turn-back or block-back assignment is a much easier block than using the guard to make the trap and the backside tackle to make a difficult cut-off block on the backside #1 defender (Diagram 5-15).

The quarterback reverses out as if he was going to ride the fullback on a belly off the left tackle. At the last moment, the ball handler slips the ball off with his right hand to the countering slotback, using an inside counter hand-off. The ball carrier follows the trapping left tackle and cuts upfield off the trapper's butt (Diagram 5-14).

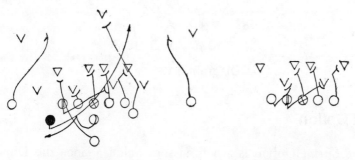

**Diagram 5-14**                         **Diagram 5-15**

## The Triple Option

With short motion, the Double Wide Slot may run the Triple Option to either side of the formation. If the defense plays hard corners—cornerbacks who are assigned to come across the line of scrimmage and attack the pitchman—the offense employs the junction block to trick these defenders to the outside. Since it is almost impossible to take the hard corner defender to the inside, we instruct the frontside slotback to release outside of the defender who is over or on his outside shoulder. He then begins to run upfield until he gets the correct angle needed to turn this hard-rushing containing cornerback to the outside. If the quarterback is able to get off the pitch, the ball carrier is coached to cut up inside of the slotback's junction block, then break to the outside to follow the split end's run-off block (Diagram 5-16).

Regular Triple Option blocking is used against the 52 Oklahoma Defense, with the frontside guard using a co-op block on the middle guard. If the center is able to block the #0 defender by himself, the guard bumps off the #0 defender and works upfield to pick off the backside 52 linebacker's pursuit course. The quarterback reads the #2 defender; if he attacks the fullback as in Diagram 5-16, the quarterback thinks "pitch." The quarterback only keeps the ball when the defensive end forces him to keep it. The quarterback pitches the ball to the trailing pitchman, and a well-executed Triple Option play is well on its way if the defensive end closes down.

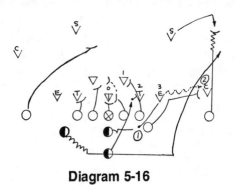

**Diagram 5-16**

## Sprint Option

The Sprint Option is a natural series choice since the Double Wide Slot Offense uses this basic backfield action for most of its passes. Since this formation spreads the defense to stop the pass, the sprint option forces the four deep defense to play honest.

The quarterback sprints straight down the line of scrimmage and options off the #3 defender. If the #3 defender attacks the quarterback, the ball handler pitches back to the trailing slotback. If the #3 defender steps to the outside and attacks the trailing slotback, the quarterback is instructed to keep the ball (Diagram 5-17).

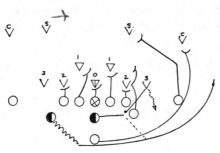

**Diagram 5-17**

The offensive players' assignments are as follows:

Frontside Split End — Block second defender to the inside.
Frontside Tackle      — #2
Frontside Guard      — #1
Center                   — #0, frontside gap, backside
Backside Guard      — Backside #1
Backside Tackle      — Backside #2
Backside Split End  — Flag

The frontside slotback blocks down and uses a co-op block. This means he helps the frontside tackle double team the #2 defender if help is needed; if not, he bumps off and picks up the shuffling inside 52 linebacker moving toward the play. The fullback leads the play and blocks the widest deep defender. The slot-back runs in motion and runs straight through the original position of the fullback. The trailing slot-back must be sure that he runs a straight (parallel to the line of scrimmage) route. Any belly or arc in his route would throw off the necessary timing of the sprint option's pitch-out.

The sprint-out may be run successfully between the quarterback and the fullback. The Sprint-Out Option has gained new success, worked within the framework of the Triple Option sequence, from the Double Wide Slot Formation. Another reason for the success of this play is that the sprint-out option looks like a sprint-out pass to the #3 defender, although the chalkboard clearly diagrams the different path of the quarterback's flat route on the sprint-out option versus the angle of the sprint-out pass. The #3 defender, during actual game conditions, over or on the outside shoulder of the frontside slotback has a difficult time distinguishing the difference between the quarterback's routes. The reader should ask his defensive ends (#3 men) about this problem. The coach should step into the end's position occasionally during an actual scrimmage encounter to portray the #3 man's defensive techniques versus the quarterback's sprint-out option and pass plays.

    *Coaching Point:* The quarterback must make sure that the slotback's short motion takes him exactly to the left halfback's normal set position when the ball is snapped from the center.

## Quarterback-Fullback Sprint-Out Option

    The Sprint-Out Option is also run between the quarterback and the fullback. The slotback swings outside to block the cornerback, while the split end is assigned to block down on the inside safetyman. The quarterback options off the #3 defender; if the end attacks, he pitches to the trailing fullback; if the #3 man shuffles outside, the quarterback runs his keeper maneuver (Diagram 5-18).

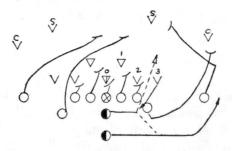

Diagram 5-18

## The Quarterback Bootleg Sprint-Out Pass

    The counter play off the sprint-out pass is a bootleg pass. A basic pass pattern against the three deep secondary is a divide pass, which strikes into the seam between the deep outside right and middle safety defenders. The man who is assigned to split this seam is the right slotback, while the left slot-back runs a hook-like pass route that often helps to screen off the middle safetyman's path to the primary receiver (Diagram 5-19).

## The Widest Double Slot Swing Pass

The Widest Slot to only one side of the formation (Diagram 5-20) forces the four deep or man-to-man defense to employ two wide secondary defenders. When these two wide defenders play the twin receivers in a man-to-man pattern, the quarterback is taught to throw the swing pass to this side. The two potential receivers are coached to run off the safety and cornerback to their side, running deep fly pass patterns. The backside slotback is assigned to run motion toward the twin set, swing behind their original positions, and take a swing pass in full flight. The receiver should catch the ball just as he begins to level off toward the line of scrimmage.

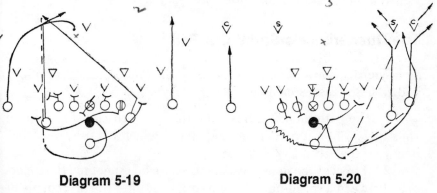

Diagram 5-19                    Diagram 5-20

The quarterback is coached to make a quick ride fake to the fullback, retreat three quick steps, and throw to the slotback.

## Wide Slot Divide Pass

Against a wide alignment, the defense may assign the outside linebacker to pick up the motion man in order to stop the Slot Swing Pass (Diagram 5-21). When this linebacker moves outside, we can run the fullback dive with cross blocks on the #1 and #2 defenders by the frontside guard and tackle. But when a pass is needed, the Divide Pass helps to exploit this man-to-man defensive secondary by running the

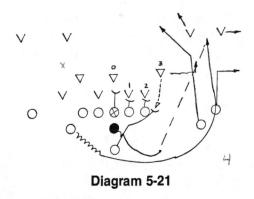

**Diagram 5-21**

swingback deep downfield, between the two wide potential pass receivers. If the defensive outside linebacker is taught to pick up the swingback, he must take him man-to-man deep downfield. This forces the linebacker to defend a fast halfback deep, which is a difficult and foreign assignment for the outside linebacker, who normally is assigned a short flat or hook zone.

## The Quarterback's Sprint-Out Path

There are several reasons for using the quarterback's sprint-out path. These reasons include:

1. The path emulates the route the quarterback uses when he runs the sprint-out option running attack, which has a holding tendency on the secondary defenders.

2. It freezes the defensive end, because he cannot tell the difference between a sprint-out pass or a sprint run after the first couple of steps by the quarterback.

3. This route helps to set up the fullback's block on the defensive #3 man, who is normally assigned to contain the run.

4. It minimizes the linebacker's proper pursuit to the run and the pass.

## The Sweep-Quarterback Throwback Pass

Against the four man-to-man secondary pass defense, the Quarterback Throwback Pass is a solid choice. By combining the slot motion with the three quick pass receivers, all four secondary pass defenders are occupied. This allows the quarterback to release into his throwback route away from the flow of the ball carrier. The fifth man release, plus the flow of the ball, usually finds the receiver open without a defender within ten yards of the quarterback (Diagram 5-22).

## The Quick Stop Pass (Widest Slot)

This is an excellent short-yardage play when the defense gangs up to stop the apparent short power run. Whenever the defense covers the widest slotback and split end with only one or one and one-half defenders (deep back and a defender in the walk-away position shown in Diagram 5-23), an automatic for the Quick Stop Pass is called. This is normally an audio-automatic to alert the screen-like blockers to help protect for the quick bullet pass.

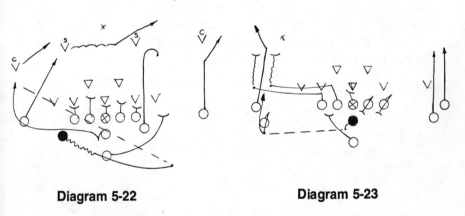

**Diagram 5-22**            **Diagram 5-23**

The passer quickly fires the ball to the slotback. The slotback takes a quick step forward as if he was releasing off the line of scrimmage, then drops back so the pass becomes a lateral. Once the slotback receives the ball, he has the option of passing the ball to his partner (split end), who runs a flag cut, or he has the option to run with the ball. If the wide defender drops back to defend against the split end, the slot man yells, "Go!" The blockers then cross the line of scrimmage and escort the slotback downfield. The success of the pass or run option maneuver forces the defense to place two to two and one-half defenders out on the flanks to stop the quick slot pass play. This type of defensive strategy opens up the running attack to the interior playside.

*Coaching Point (Widest Slot):* The "Widest Slot" refers to the slotback who is split outside of the offensive tackle ten or more yards. The twin wide receivers help to further stretch the Double Wide Slot Offense. The "Widest" alignment is primarily used to the wide side of the field, to one or both sides of the center. These widest players are normally referred to as twins.

## Double Wide Slot Pull-Up Passes

The Split End Delay Pass (Diagram 5-24) has a high completion consistency, whether the defense is in a man-to-man pass defense (Diagram 5-24) or in a zone roll (Diagram 5-25).

Diagram 5-24 illustrates the delayed come-back pass pattern by the split right end coming back into the open area after the offensive fullback and slotback have run off the two deep man-to-man secondary defenders. In Diagram 5-25, versus the rolling secondary or Cloud coverage, the fullback's running a seam or crease cut and/or the delayed come-back split end's pattern may pop open against the re-volving defensive secondary.

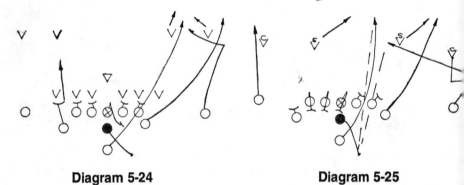

Diagram 5-24                          Diagram 5-25

Some defenses using four deep pass coverage will favor an invert or Sky type of revolving secondary which assigns the inside safety to cover the flat, the outside cornerman to cover the deep middle, and the backside safety to defend the deep middle one-third area (Diagram 5-26). Again, the fullback and the delayed split end work themselves into the open area as we have seen in Diagram 5-25.

Against the locked-in three deep 52 Monster Defense, the quick side-out at eight yards by the wide receiver away from the Monster defender has been a successful pass. The quarterback calls the play, lines up, and calls an automatic to run it to the side away from the

Monster. The deep one-third defender away from the Monster is then placed in a pressure situation. The slotback runs a deep cut, and the wide receiver runs a quick, eight-yard sideline pattern. There is no way the defensive alignment can defend this pass, as illustrated in Diagram 5-27.

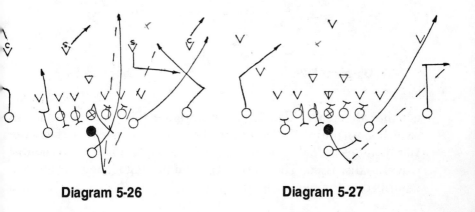

Diagram 5-26                              Diagram 5-27

## How to Defeat the Defensive Trailer

The "trailer" is the defender who plays the motioning slotback man-to-man wherever he goes.

Whenever we see the trailer running across the formation, we like to go back to the weak side. Since the trailer causes his direction side of the formation to be strongly unbalanced, the side of the formation on which he originally lined up becomes the weak side of the formation.

The Drag Pass to the right slotback or the Look-In Pass (dotted line) to the left split end are both strategic passes for taking advantage of the defensive trailer (Diagram 5-28).

A belly tackle trap is a fine running play for taking advantage of the defensive trailer as he leaves his original position. Diagram 5-29 shows a successful trap on the defensive #4 man with a counter action hand-off to the backside slotback. Regardless of whether the defensive #4 man moves to his inside, over the outside shoulder of the left offensive tackle, the trap is an excellent choice to stop the trailer from following the motioning slotback.

A most important offensive attack is described in the following chapter. Studying the Wishbone Formation is of great importance,

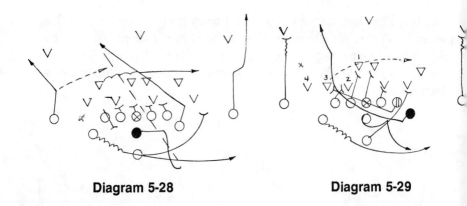

**Diagram 5-28**                              **Diagram 5-29**

whether the reader decides to incorporate this formation into his offensive planning or whether the reader expects to face the Wishbone in his fall schedule. The Triple Option and its sequential plays are discussed. The more successful passing maneuvers are also described in the next chapter.

# 6

# THE WISHBONE FORMATION

## How the Wishbone Will Help You Win

The Wishbone Formation features the Triple Option maneuver, which allows the offense the option of striking at three points of attack along the line of scrimmage after the ball has been put into play. The balanced line and full-house backfield allow the offense to mirror itself to either side of the center. Speed and power are two of the most important assets of the Wishbone attack. All four of the backs have an equal chance to carry the ball; thus, the Wishbone is normally a balanced offensive attack. The split end provides a break-away threat for the passing attack, while the tight end and the backs sliding out of the backfield help to undermine the defense via the short and medium passes.

The flexibility of the dive, quarterback keep, and the pitch-out gives the Triple Option a three-way offensive striking force. Play-action passes off the Triple Option series help to keep the defense honest in its respect of the passing potential of the Wishbone Offense.

## The Advantages of the Wishbone Formation

1. The Wishbone is a four-back offense with any one of the backs having the break-away potential on any down or distance situation.
2. The offensive goal line attack is the same attack that is featured from goal line to goal line.
3. Simplicity is the key to the Wishbone Formation. Seventy percent of all plays should be the basic Triple Option plays.
4. The Triple Option holds up the defense's pursuit since this play has the ability of hitting three points of attack along the line of scrimmage. This means a minimum of eight defenders (three versus the run, one versus the pass to each side of the center) must be assigned to stop the Triple Option.
5. The Triple Option series has the advantage of reading the defense on the run. This means the quarterback has the ability to read the defensive strategy while the play is in progress.
6. The Wishbone may split both ends to each side of the line and still run the regular full house backfield set.
7. Power is derived from the Drive Series, which features the key block by the frontside halfback.
8. The split end gives the passing attack a continual long bomb threat.
9. This offense forces each halfback to strive to be a complete football player. This means the halfback must be a runner, faker, pass receiver, and a blocker.
10. The continual Triple Option running threat helps to emphasize the success of the play-action passing attack.

## The Basic Wishbone Formation's Alignment

The fullback lines up in a four-point stance, four yards away from the center. The fullback should be in a straight line with the center and the quarterback. The halfback's width and depth must be consistent on all Triple Option plays to keep the faking and timing consistent.

The split end is assigned to split out approximately ten yards. The tight end's split varies between two to three feet. All of the other interior linemen are instructed to use a minimum two-foot split (Diagram 6-1).

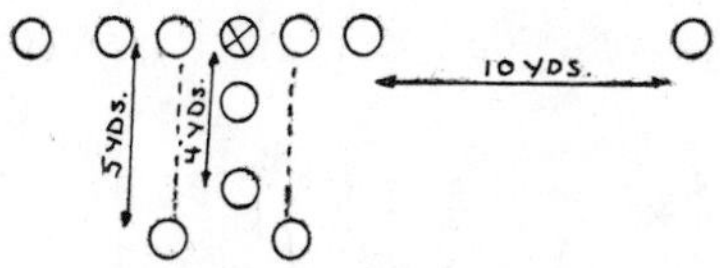

Diagram 6-1

## The Wishbone's Triple Option Guide

The philosophy of the Wishbone's Triple Option attack is to get to the outside and turn the opponent's corner. This means we teach our quarterbacks to get the pitch off whenever possible.

Getting outside quickly is accomplished by running the Triple Option, Triple Block (Load), Veer Option, and Sprint-Out Option.

In order to keep the interior defenders honest and to keep the outside option game, the fullback give, halfback counter, cut, and halfback "X" plays help out the wide plays by holding these defenders.

Whenever the defensive ends play a holding, soft, or penetrating technique, the fullback veers, halfback veer, and drive plays are called. These quick-diving thrusts force the wide defenders to pinch inside to stop these maneuvers. Thus, these inside moves help to set up the defensive flanks for the outside Triple Option plays.

Throwback passes and counter option plays are unleashed versus the fast-revolving or rotating defensive secondaries.

*Coaching Point (Triple Block)*: The Triple Block or Load play assigns the lead halfback to block the defender responsible for tackling the quarterback.

## The Wishbone Triple Option Play

Basically the offensive linemen are assigned to seal off the interior defenders. The two outside defenders on or just off the line of scrimmage are not blocked. The fullback runs into the crease, setting a course for the outside foot of the frontside offensive guard. The quarterback is instructed to give the ball to the fullback if the #2 defender (Diagram 6-2) steps across the line of scrimmage. If the #2 defender attacks the diving fullback, the quarterback pulls the ball out of the fullback's pocket and continues his parallel path down the line. The second key for the quarterback is the #3 man. The #3

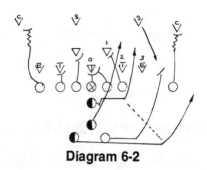

**Diagram 6-2**

defender is referred to as the *pitch key*. This means that if the #3 man attacks the quarterback, he must pitch the ball to the trailing halfback. If the #3 key steps across the line of scrimmage or feathers to his outside to stop the pitch-out, the quarterback is instructed to keep the ball and run his prescribed keeper play. Thus, the three phases of the Triple Option are: 1) give the ball to the diving fullback, 2) keep the ball on the keeper play, or 3) pitch the ball back to the trailing left halfback on the pitch-out maneuver.

The primary objective of the Triple Option is to isolate the first (dive) key (#2 defender), then attack the second (pitch-keep) key (#3 defender). Because of the position of the fullback ride, most Triple Option Wishbone attacks favor a double team block on the middle guard (#0 defender).

## The Fullback Give

The quarterback is coached to give the ball to the diving fullback whenever the first key (#2 area) does not attack the fullback. In Diagram 6-3, the #2 linebacker in the Eagle Defense loops to the outside, which creates a space outside of the offensive tackle's block. Therefore, the quarterback gives the ball to the fullback.

## The Quarterback Keeper

Whenever the #2 man attacks the fullback, the quarterback disconnects from the fullback and keeps the ball. He then reads the next key, which is the #3 defender. If this defender steps outside to stop the pitch-out or feathers to the outside, the quarterback keeps the ball by pushing off his back foot and turning upfield on the keeper play (Diagram 6-4).

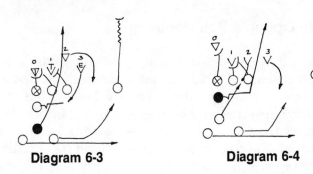

Diagram 6-3           Diagram 6-4

## The Pitch-Out

The pitch-out versus the 52 Defense has been demonstrated in Diagram 6-2. The pitch-out is made when the #3 defender attacks the quarterback (Diagram 6-5).

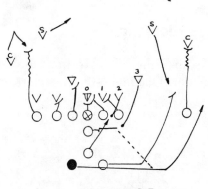

Diagram 6-5

## Quarterback's Triple Option Steps

While the quarterback is taught a few basic steps of the mesh to the dive man, he is not taught to use a specific number of steps in the ride, keep, or pitch phases of the Triple Option. All quarterbacks are different in mannerisms, size, and speed. Therefore, the quarterback is told approximately where the crease should be and then he should be left on his own! This makes the quarterback's fakes and footwork more natural, pertaining to his own physical and mental talents. Regardless of the speed or quickness of the ball handler, he must be continually under control to be able to make whatever play the defense gives him.

## The Triple Option's Ball Handling

The dive back is assigned to take a course just outside of the far foot of the frontside or playside offensive guard. In the first phase of the Triple Option, the quarterback is coached to give the ball to the dive back if the first defender outside of the offensive tackle's block does not attack the dive back. If this defender attacks the dive back, the quarterback is instructed to keep the ball and continue down the line of scrimmage. If the next defender to show does not attack the quarterback, the ball handler is taught to keep the ball and turn upfield on the keeper—this is the second phase of the Triple Option. If this defender attacks the quarterback, he is assigned to pitch the ball out to the trailing back to complete phase three of the Triple Option maneuver. Put these three phases together, and you have the Triple Option attack.

## Triple Option Base Blocking

Base blocking features the offensive frontside tackle's assigned block on the #2 defender (Diagram 6-6). The quarterback places the

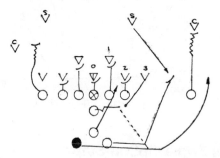

**Diagram 6-6**

ball into the fullback's pocket and either gives the ball to him or keeps it. If he keeps the ball, the quarterback reads the space beyond the offensive tackle's block. If there is space, the quarterback keeps the ball and turns upfield to run his keeper play. If the #3 defender attacks the quarterback, he pitches the ball to the backside trailing halfback. The lead halfback blocks the inverting safety, and the split end executes his run off block on the widest outside deep defender.

## Triple Option Blocking Versus
## The 52 Defense

Normally the Triple Option blocks the 52 Defense as demonstrated in Diagram 6-7. But many defensive teams began to close the defensive tackle down with the inside movement of the offensive tackle. This means the #2 defender started to stuff the fullback quickly, deep in the offensive backfield.

One offensive method of stopping the defensive tackle's penetration is to block him. This means the Triple Option is no longer a true Triple Option, because the quarterback is now only reading space (rather than the man) outside of the offensive tackle's block (Diagram 6-8). This is normally referred to as *base blocking*.

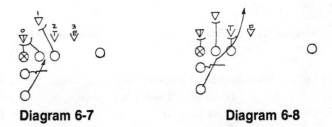

| Diagram 6-7 | Diagram 6-8 |

Another method of delaying the defensive tackle's quick closing technique is to step the offensive tackle around or to the outside of the #2 man. This holds the defensive tackle just long enough so the offensive tackle can block the scalloping #1 linebacker.

Diagram 6-9 illustrates how the looping tackle helps to double team the outstanding defensive linebacker. As long as the center is able to handle the middle guard by utilizing his one-on-one block, this blocking technique is a solid choice.

Another method of cutting off the quick scrapping or scalloping 52 linebacker is to teach the offensive guard to step around the offen-

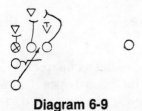

Diagram 6-9

sive tackle's block. This blocking scheme is particularly effective against the frontside linebacker, who likes to slant into the gap between the frontside guard and tackle (Diagram 6-10).

If the frontside linebacker scrapes to the outside and the defensive tackle slants to the inside, the offensive tackle must take the slanting defensive tackle. This means the frontside tackle blocks the #2 man and the step-around frontside guard blocks the #1 defender (Diagram 6-11). The offensive pulling or step-around guard must first

    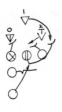

**Diagram 6-10**                    **Diagram 6-11**

check to make sure that the defensive #1 man is not going to barrel directly over the frontside guard's original position (Diagram 6-12).

The step-around blocking technique must teach the offensive tackle to continue to drive down inside if the inside defensive linebacker shuffles or scrapes too quickly around the offensive blocker's inside path. This means the tackle continues inside and looks for the scalloping backside 52 linebacker (Diagram 6-13). This step-around blocking technique is nothing more than a cross block between the offensive frontside guard and tackle.

**Diagram 6-12**                    **Diagram 6-13**

Regardless of the blocking technique used by the frontside offensive guard and tackle, the offensive center must always step to the frontside (playside) whenever he is coached to block the #0 man one-on-one.

At times, the frontside offensive tackle is not able to drive inside and get his normal angle to block the 52 inside linebacker. When this defense occurs (the frontside defensive tackle aligns head-up on the frontside offensive tackle), the offensive tackle is coached to step around the #2 defender, then curl back and block the #1 defender. The success of the frontside tackle's curl block is determined by the technique of the frontside offensive guard. The offensive guard is taught to step up and check the #1 linebacker before he helps double team the #0 man. This means that if the #1 defender decides to blitz, the frontside offensive guard would block the blitzing linebacker with a one-on-one block (Diagram 6-14).

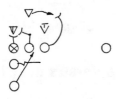

**Diagram 6-14**

## Triple Option Versus
## The 65 Goal Line Defense

Since many defensive 65 teams use the frontside safetyman as the tackler responsible for stopping the quarterback, the Triple Option play often results in a keeper play versus this defense. Diagram 6-15 illustrates the tight end blocking down on the inside frontside defensive safetyman. As soon as the quarterback disconnects from the dive back, he is coached to keep the ball, push off his back foot, then turn upfield and head for the end zone.

If the defensive #4 man (the safety is counted as the #3 defender

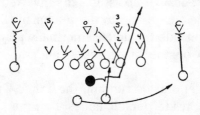

**Diagram 6-15**

because he is close to the line of scrimmage on or near the goal line) attacks the quarterback, the quarterback is told to pitch the ball. Diagram 6-16 shows the #4 defender veering to attack the quarter-back, who then pitches the ball back to the backside offensive halfback.

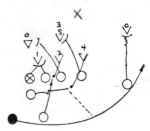

**Diagram 6-16**

## Wishbone Principles Versus the 52 Defense

1. If the ball is in the center of the field, split both ends versus the 52 Monster Defense. Now the quarterback can call an automatic to run the Triple Option away from the overshifted Monster's side.

2. If the 52 employs a basic three deep secondary, use the normal one split end to the wide side of field.

3. If the 52 uses a balanced four deep, split both ends. This forces the secondary to play basically an invert pass defense to both sides.

4. Throw post passes and curls versus an inverting secondary. Hit the receiver beyond the invert in the seam.

5. Run a cut play if the 52 linebacker moves out to help on the split side (Diagram 6-17).

6. Against the invert defense, the defensive invert is assigned to the pitchman, the defensive end tackles the quarterback, and the tackle takes the dive back.

7. One invert change-up assigns the inverted safety to the quarterback and the defensive end to the pitchman (Diagram 6-18).

8. To the tight side the defense normally plays the tackle on the fullback, the end on the quarterback, and the cornerback on the pitchman.

9. Work to get outside running the Triple Option.

10. Keep the inside pursuit honest by running the fullback give play.

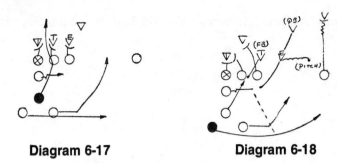

Diagram 6-17                              Diagram 6-18

11. If the linebackers are overpursuing to the outside, run quick dives, the Cut play, and halfback counters directly at the linebacker's area.

12. The Outside Veer to the tight end's side is effective because it helps to confuse the defensive end's normal Triple Option assignments.

13. Also run the counter option play to the tight end's side.

14. Have the ends run an occasional fly cut to keep the deep defenders honest and deep pass conscious.

## Wishbone Principles Versus the 44 Defense

1. If the middle safetyman plays at a shallow depth, the offense should split both ends to their maximum splits. The Wishbone attack should then throw into the seams, use throwback passes, and run counter option and scissors plays.

2. Maximum splits by both ends minimize the revolving or rotation of the three deep secondary.

3. Feature the fullback dive play to the tight end's side along with the quarterback's keep-pitch block or load technique.

4. Work to get the pitch off to the split end's side.

5. Call an automatic for the quick look-in pass versus the three deep secondary.

6. Large splits by the offensive tackles help to stretch out the eight man front.

7. The Wishbone attack must work to isolate the inside four, the defensive tackles and inside linebackers, and minimize their pursuit patterns.

8. Most 44 teams put the #1 inside linebacker and the #2 defensive tackle on the fullback. Thus, the quarterback and lead back on

the Triple Option must read the #3 and #4 defenders (Diagram 6-19).

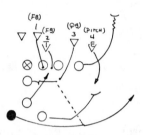

**Diagram 6-19**

9. The backside tackle must be blocked at all times to eliminate his backside pursuit.

10. Keep the tight end's defensive side honest by running the halfback veer and the drive play.

11. The quick hitting halfback counter and dives will help hold and isolate the interior four defenders.

## Wishbone Triple Option Interior Blocking Multi-Inside 44 Looks

Against the stacked 44 "look," the fold block between the frontside guard and tackle is a must. This call is made by the offensive frontside tackle, because he realizes he does not have the proper angle to block the #2 defender (Diagram 6-20).

The fold block is also a natural call versus the defensive tackle (#2) who favors the outside loop technique. Whenever the tackle favors the outside loop, the frontside offensive guard must use a cautious fold. This means the guard must be cautious, looking for an inside blitz by the #1 defender into the gap between the center and himself. As soon as the guard insures against the possible blitz, he folds around the offensive tackle's drive block and cuts off the #1 defender's scrape technique.

Diagram 6-21 illustrates a White call by the frontside tackle which features a double team block by the frontside guard and tackle on the #2 defender. This call is made whenever the center has a good chance of cutting down the #1 linebacker. The two-time block is coached to drive the defensive tackle (#2) straight back upfield, with the potential of cutting off the interior defensive linebacker's pursuit path.

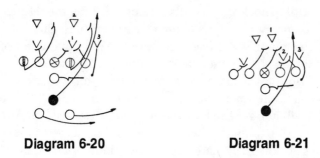

Diagram 6-20                    Diagram 6-21

## Wishbone Load Play Destroys the 44 Defense

The one specific play that has ruined more 44 defenses is the Wishbone Load maneuver. Diagram 6-22 points out the excellent blocking angles of the backside tackle and guard, the center and the faking fullback. The two-time block by the frontside guard and tackle destroys the defensive 44 tackle. The frontside halfback is assigned to overthrow on the #3 defender, who has been set up by the quarterback's ride fake and his path parallel to the line of scrimmage. If the #4 man defends against the possible pitch-out, the quarterback merely keeps the ball and runs the keeper play.

If the #2 defender chooses to tackle the quarterback, the pitch-out is made and the tight end uses his run-off block on the deep outside defender.

The key to Diagram 6-22 is that the load call alerts the fullback that he is primarily a blocker and not a faker. This allows the dive back to sprint out into the crease and cut off the inside frontside 44

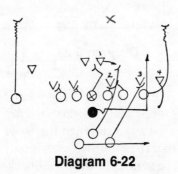

Diagram 6-22

linebacker. The fullback's block, along with the double team block by the frontside guard and tackle, helps to seal off the 44 Defense's interior players.

The Triple Block play is often referred to as the Triple Option Load play by many members of the coaching profession. The "Block" or "Load" means that the lead back in the Wishbone Offense blocks the defender responsible for tackling the quarterback.

The Triple Block is a predetermined pitch or keeper by the quarterback. Whenever this play has been called, the fullback realizes he will *not* get the ball and is primarily a blocker. Versus the 44 Defense, the fullback checks to block the inside pursuit, then heads straight downfield and blocks the middle safetyman.

## Triple Block (Load) Versus the 52 Defense

When running the Triple Block (Load) play to the split end's side against the 52 Defense, the lead back is assigned to block the defender responsible for tackling the quarterback. In Diagram 6-23 the dive fullback is tackled by the #2 defender. The lead halfback is taught to block the #3 man, who is responsible for tackling the quarterback. The quarterback is told to keep his eyes on the first defender to show outside of the lead back's block. If the safetyman attacks the quarterback, the quarterback pitches the ball to the trailing halfback.

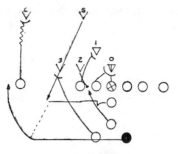

**Diagram 6-23**

Naturally, if the safetyman attacks the pitchman, the quarterback keeps the ball. The keeper play, as executed by the quarterback to the tight end's side, is easier to run than the basic Triple Option play. The reason for this is that the quarterback has only two options—keep or pitch—because there is no give to the fullback on the Triple Block play.

*Coaching Point*: One of the major reasons for selecting the Triple Block play is to protect the quarterback. Certainly the defensive end has a clear shot at the quarterback in the 52 Defense. Blocking the defender responsible for the quarterback helps to keep the quarterback in the game longer, with less chance of incurring damaging injuries.

## Outside Halfback Veer

Whenever the Outside Halfback Veer Play (Diagram 6-24) has been called, the diving halfback is taught to receive the ball from the quarterback and go for the outside foot of the blocking frontside offensive tackle. Emphasis must be placed on receiving the ball *first*, then on the ball carrier making his cut. All too often, the diving halfback runs too wide at the start of the play, and the quarterback is unable to hand the ball off to the diving halfback.

The quarterback must accelerate down the line of scrimmage, faking the second and third phases of the Veer to hold the #4 defender to the outside. The tight end is coached to block the #3 defender head-on. Since the #3 man is normally assigned to stop the dive, he usually steps to his inside, so the tight end blocks the defender in that direction.

*Coaching Point*: The Outside Halfback Veer play's dive is not as exaggerated as illustrated in Diagram 6-24, because the #3 man normally steps inside and the diving ball carrier's dive route is a straighter course.

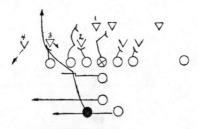

**Diagram 6-24**

## Auxiliary Halfback Outside Veer

The Halfback Veer is designated a pitch-out as soon as the cornerback (#4) closes down and attacks the quarterback (Diagram 6-25).

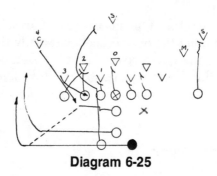

**Diagram 6-25**

The #4 defender is forced into attacking the quarterback as soon as the #3 man steps inside and tackles the diving veer halfback. Once the pitch has been made, the ball carrier is led downfield by the lead-blocking fullback. Once he clears the line of scrimmage, the lead halfback is coached to block the deep middle one-third defender.

## The Fullback Cut Play

The Fullback Cut Play is a cut-back play all the way; normally, the ball carrier cuts back behind the defensive middle guard. The fullback is instructed to run the frontside guard-center gap. The quarterback must be able to adjust his feet because of the quick moves and cuts required of him. All of the other members of the backfield use their normal Triple Option backfield action (Diagram 6-26).

At times, the fullback will run the cut play behind the rapidly pursuing backside linebacker in the 52 Defense.

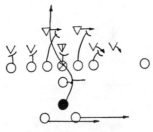

**Diagram 6-26**

## Drive Versus the 44 Defense

One unique method of blocking the 44 Defense is to execute a fold block by the frontside guard and tackle and double team the #3 defender (Diagram 6-27). The double team block is applied by the tight end as the post man and the inside-out-blocking fullback as the drive man. The tight end is coached to hold his block until he feels the fullback's drive block, then he releases downfield to block the deep outside defensive back. Since this drive play looks like the Triple Option backfield action, the frontside halfback runs his normal lead route. The lead route helps to set up the outside linebacker for the two-time block and influences the #4 defender away from the point of the attack. The quarterback is taught to make a quick ride to the fullback, then hand the ball off to the ball carrier. Once the hand-off has been accomplished, the quarterback is assigned to drop back and fake setting up for a pass.

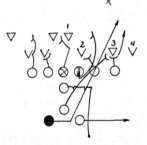

**Diagram 6-27**

*Coaching Point*: The tight end is coached to take a maximum split whenever the man over or outside defender moves outside with his split. This takes the defender farther from the point of the attack, creating a natural hole for the drive play.

## The Importance of
## The Wishbone Counter Plays

Since most defensive teams try to get the extra defender into the pursuit pattern to stop the Triple Option Pitch, and many defensive teams attempt to shut off the quarterback keeper phase of the Triple Option with defensive flow, the counter plays are the all-important maneuvers for minimizing the defensive pursuit.

The Halfback Counter, Inside Counter, and the Counter Option are three important offensive plays that are specifically designed to cut down pursuit. These misdirection plays are designed to force the defense to move in one direction and to pop the ball carrier free in the opposite direction. The Triple Option helps make the counter play a successful long gainer. Conversely, the counter plays help make the Triple Option plays more successful. The most important phases of the counter plays are described and illustrated in the following pages.

## The Halfback Counter

The Halfback Counter is an excellent supplement to the Triple Option play. This inside counter starts out exactly like a Triple Option play, but hits with speed and deception to the opposite side of the backfield flow. Against fast-flowing linebackers, the Inside Counter is a highly successful call.

Basically, the Halfback Counter is run to the tight end's side of the line. Since most Wishbone teams like to run their Triple Option plays to the split end's side of the line, this quick-hitting counter maneuver also takes advantage of fast-pursuing defensive secondaries.

Diagram 6-28 features a fold block at the point of the attack versus the 62 Defense. The left tackle is assigned to block down on the #1 man, while the left offensive guard uses a fold-blocking technique and blocks down on the influenced #2 (inside-shuffling) linebacker. The ball carrier cuts off the tail of the frontside offensive guard's fold block on the #2 linebacker.

An inside fold block by the frontside offensive tackle on the frontside #1 linebacker in the 44 Defense helps to spring the diving ball carrier. The frontside left guard must turn out on the #2 defender until the ball carrier has cleared the point of the attack. The quick-hitting Halfback Trap is an excellent call versus quick-scrapping and shuffling inside linebackers in the 44 Defense (Diagram 6-29).

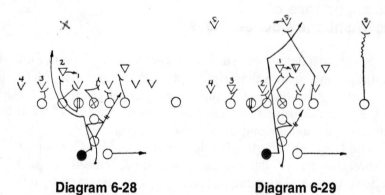

**Diagram 6-28**　　　　　　　　　　**Diagram 6-29**

## Alternative Blocking
## For the Halfback Counter

Another excellent method of blocking the Halfback Counter Play is to use an inside fold block by the frontside offensive tackle. The frontside offensive guard has a good angle on the frontside #2 defender. The frontside linebacker begins to move to his right to stop the offensive backfield flow; from the backside, the frontside tackle is able to drive the #1 defender away from the point of the attack. All of the other blockers execute their normal one-on-one blocks. The ball carrier is coached to break opposite the offensive tackle's key block (Diagram 6-30).

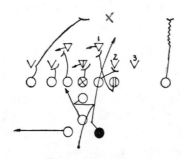

Diagram 6-30

## Halfback Inside Counter

One of the finest and newest Wishbone plays is the Halfback Inside Counter Play. This play is particularly successful versus the fast-scrapping 44 inside linebackers. A quick fake to the diving fullback makes this play similar to the normal Triple Option play, only at the last moment the quarterback stops, pulls back his front foot, and slips the ball off to the right halfback. The right halfback is coached to take a quick lead step with his lead foot (to his right), then cut off the inside foot of the center's original position. The offensive guards use turn-out blocks to screen off the #2 defenders. The center blocks the frontside linebacker in the direction the #1 defender wants to go. The backside offensive halfback takes a lead step with his inside foot toward the frontside, then pushes off this foot to block the backside inside linebacker. The left halfback blocks this backside #1 man any way the defender chooses to go. Diagram 6-31 points out two cuts the ball carrier may select. These cuts are determined by the flow of the inside linebackers. Against quick-moving linebackers, the best cut normally finds the ball carrier cutting behind the shuffling backside linebacker.

Diagram 6-32 shows the Halfback Inside Counter against the 52 Oklahoma Defense. The left guard uses a co-op block on the middle guard. If the center can take the #0 man by himself, the left guard continues to the next target and blocks the right 52 inside linebacker. The left tackle turns outside and screens off the defensive tackle. The left halfback uses his isolation or blast block on the right inside linebacker. The fullback fakes his normal triple route and blocks the left defensive tackle. The ball carrier makes the same cut as in Diagram 6-31 and sprints for daylight (Diagram 6-32).

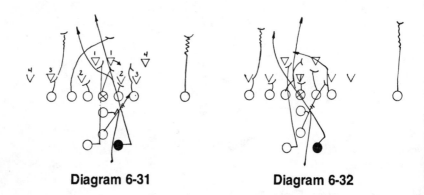

**Diagram 6-31**                    **Diagram 6-32**

## Counter Option Versus the 52 Defense

The Counter Option Play (Diagram 6-33) is a fine choice to the tight end's side. This play helps to minimize the deep secondary's

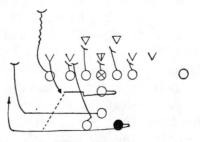

**Diagram 6-33**

fast-revolving or rotating deep backs. The quick reverse pivot by the quarterback and the stutter steps by both offensive halfbacks help to hold the interior defenders long enough to enable the counter option to get around the corner.

Key coaching points that make this play a long gainer are:

1. The dive halfback must cheat his alignment to the outside so he may dive at the inside foot of the #2 defender. This forces the #2 man to hold and tackle the faking dive back.

2. The fullback runs a straight course parallel to the line of scrimmage and begins to break upfield after his fifth step. The five steps are used (rather than the three steps by the lead halfback on the normal Triple Option play) because of the delay of the Counter Option play. It is basically run to the tight end's side; this means the extra offensive linemen make the blocker run further parallel to get to the containing secondary defender.

3. The tight end blocks the second deep defender to the inside. The blocker makes the defender come to him. Thus, the tight end is coached to shuffle up to a point where he can screen off the defender's pursuit path.

4. The quarterback must be ready to pitch immediately after he pivots, as some defensive ends will crash down on him at the snap of the ball. If the defensive end steps outside, the quarterback is coached to keep the ball and look for the inside #1 linebacker or inside safetyman to attack him as he turns upfield.

## Counter Option Versus the 44 Defense

Against the fast-rotating or revolving three deep secondary defense, the Counter Option Play is an excellent choice. The quarterback starts toward the split end side, then reverse pivots and starts down the line toward his tight end. This misdirection move helps to freeze the inside four defenders. If the #3 defender holds on the line of scrimmage, the quarterback is coached to hand the ball off to the diving halfback as demonstrated in Diagram 6-34.

If the #3 defender tackles the dive halfback, the quarterback is coached to keep the ball and turn upfield, running his keeper play.

If the #3 man tackles the dive halfback and the #4 defender attacks the quarterback, the quarterback is instructed to pitch the ball to the trailing halfback on the last phase of the Counter Option Play.

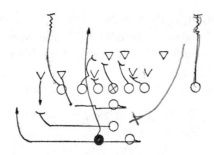

**Diagram 6-34**

## Breaking the Wishbone

There are advantageous times when the Wishbone Offense may wish to break up its three-back attack and run a two-back slot attack. One reason is its effectiveness against an opponent who plays a corner defense to the tight end side and an invert set to the slot side. Against this secondary alignment, a natural passing attack may be formulated to the slot side of the formation. The three defenders are (Diagram 6-35):

*First*: What is the alignment of the free or backside safetyman? If he aligns to the tight end side, stay in the Wish-Slot alignment.

*Second*: What is the invert defender's assignment on the drop-back pass? If he takes the flat, stay in the Wish-Slot alignment.

*Third*: How does the deep defender play his wide one-third zone? If he plays the deep one-third, run the Wish-Slot attack.

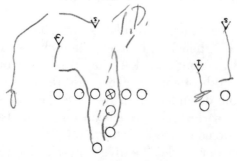

**Diagram 6-35**

## The Wish-Slot Passing Attack

The Split End Post Cut is an excellent pass call with the slotback running a flat cut. The slotback takes the invert defender into the flat

zone and the split end runs a post pattern into the open crease between the middle and the deep left pass defenders (Diagram 6-36).

The Split End Curl is another pass pattern that takes advantage
of the open right passing seam. The slotback runs a swing pass pattern
into the flat area, and the split end runs a curl pass. The curling
receiver slides to his right or left to get open, always sliding away from
the dropping defensive linebacker (Diagram 6-37).

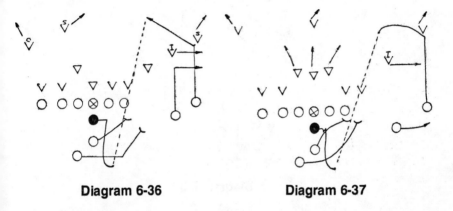

Diagram 6-36                          Diagram 6-37

Flying the slotback and running the split end into the flat is
another double wide-out pass pattern that takes advantage of the
invert pass defense. Now the invert defender and the deep outside
safetyman are placed in a precarious secondary position (Diagram
6-38). The slot's fly pass pattern cuts off the invert's flat course, which
frees the split end's sideline cut. If the invert can get out to the flat
area, the passer is coached to hit the slotback on a deep fly pass
pattern. This is especially true if the deep left safetyman plays his
deep outside one-third zone (Diagram 6-38).

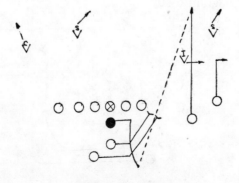

Diagram 6-38

If the deep outside safety does not go to his outside one-third zone and slides over to help cover the slotback running his fly pattern through the seam, the split end runs the second phase of his sideline cut—the up pass pattern as illustrated in Diagram 6-39. Now the passer throws the sideline-and-up pass to the split end, and it looks like "deep six!" (Diagram 6-39).

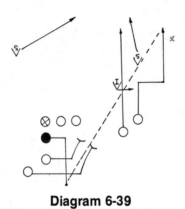

**Diagram 6-39**

## The Wish-Slot Running Attack

The Sprint-Out Option helps to keep the four deep pass defenders honest. Now the offensive backs merely continue their run-pass action and attack the corner with the pitch-keep running maneuver. The outside duo execute their run-off blocks while the quarterback sprints directly at the #3 defender. If the #3 man attacks the quarterback, he pitches, and away goes the ball carrier with an added (fullback) blocker. If the #3 defender steps outside to stop the pitchman, the quarterback keeps the ball and runs the Quarterback Keeper Play (Diagram 6-40).

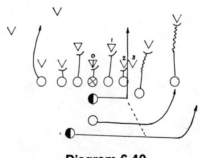

**Diagram 6-40**

The Triple Option is another fine running maneuver off the broken Wishbone Formation, particularly when it is run to the slot's side versus the 52 Defense. If the #2 man tackles the fullback, the quarterback pulls the ball out of the diving fullback's pocket. Next the quarterback challenges the #3 defender. If the #3 defender attacks the quarterback, he pitches the ball out to the trailing halfback to complete the third phase of the Triple Option play. As seen in Diagram 6-40, the two wide potential receivers are assigned to use their run-off blocks on the two wide defenders. Since this is the Triple Option play, all of the interior defenders are sealed off to the inside. With the offensive center and frontside guard two-timing the #0 defender, the frontside offensive tackle seals off the #1 defender.

## Pop Pass

The Pop Pass (Diagram 6-41) is an excellent call, especially to the short side of the field. This means that if the opposition is running a 52

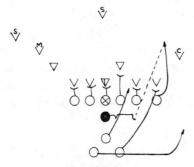

**Diagram 6-41**

Monster Defense against the Wishbone attack, the tight end is normally free. The fake to the fullback into the crease holds the frontside defensive linebacker. All of the offensive linemen are coached to fire out, emulating a normal Wishbone running play. Additionally, the offensive linemen are taught to fire out low, which forces the defensive linemen to bring their hands down to ward off the scramble blocking techniques. The deep outside secondary defender to the tight end's side must gain width to stop the potential Triple Option pitch-out threat. This gives the tight end an open corridor between the middle safety and the defensive cornerback.

Immediately after the dive fake, the quarterback is coached to plant his right foot and direct the pass toward the tight end's numbers.

## Play-Action Protection Versus
## The 44 Defense

Maximum protection versus the Split-Forty Defense is a must, because this eight man front has a history of stunting and blitzing all eight defenders. This means the offense must dispatch four blockers to both the front and back sides to account for these eight potential rushers. Diagram 6-42 illustrates blocking on the front or play side with two offensive backs and the frontside tackle and guard. The four blockers assigned to pick up the backside potential rushers include: the center, backside guard, tackle, and the halfback. This allows both the split end and the tight end to be potential receivers. The frontside halfback may also be a receiver if the frontside defensive end or linebacker does not rush.

*Coaching Point*: The frontside offensive tackle is coached to block the first rusher who shows to his outside. This means that if only one man rushes, the tackle will block him, freeing the frontside halfback to be a receiver (Diagram 6-42).

The Halfback Throwback Pass is blocked as featured in Diagram 6-43. The tight end is called upon to block the man over, with the lead halfback assigned to block the next outside rusher.

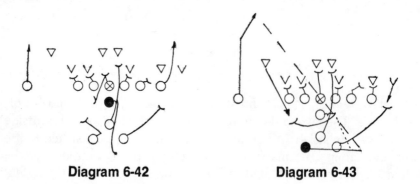

Diagram 6-42                              Diagram 6-43

## Play-Action Protection Versus
## The Seven Man Front

The basic pass protection off running action against the seven man front is demonstrated in Diagram 6-44. All of the offensive linemen use their normal, low fire-out blocking, with the backside guard checking the Oklahoma backside linebacker. If this defender drops back to defend against the pass, the blocker is coached to drop back and pick up any possible backside outside rush.

If we face the 61 Defense, the center becomes the check blocker. Whenever the middle linebacker does not blitz, the center is taught to shuffle backward and check the outside backside rush (Diagram 6-44).

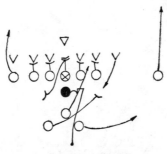

Diagram 6-44

## Not All Pass Defenses End Up Three Deep

Many Wishbone coaches who tell their quarterbacks to always throw against three deep secondary pass defenses are incorrect. These coaches have taught their quarterbacks that the three deep or four deep secondaries will always revolve into a three deep zone pass defense. This is a false premise for three reasons:

*First*: Several defenses are playing straight three or four deep, man-to-man pass defenses.

*Second*: Many coaches play the nine man front defense with the two deep safeties playing man-to-man on the Wishbone's tight and split ends.

*Third*: Some defenses are now using a four-man rush, five underneath run-pass defenders, and two deep safeties playing one-half deep zones respectively.

## Tight End Post Throwback Pass

The Post Pass (Diagram 6-45) is an excellent pass against a fast-revolving four deep secondary. A quick ride to the fullback, the lead back's block on the #3 defender, and the first two steps of the left halfback make the throw-back pass resemble a Triple Option toward the split end. As soon as the quarterback makes a good mesh with the fullback, he is instructed to drop back, set up, and look toward the split end's flag route. The passer then focuses his attention on the tight end and delivers the ball just as the post receiver makes his break and as the right defensive safetyman sprints to cover his deep middle one-third assignment. When executed properly, the Tight End Post Throw-back Pass is one of the Wishbone's most successful touchdown pass plays.

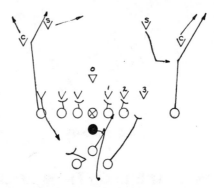

**Diagram 6-45**

## Drive-Backfield Action Pass Blocking

Drive-backfield action pass protection is a solid choice when running a pass play toward the 52 Monster man. This means the lead back is now free to run a flare pass pattern, which enables the offense to clear the Monster out of the passing lane and allows the passer to throw a curl pass to the split end without an obstruction (Diagram 6-46).

## If the Split End Is Double Covered

Although there are few times when the split end is double covered, the quarterback is encouraged to give the ball to the fullback. The strategy behind this premise is that the #2 defender must focus his attention mentally and physically on the quarterback. If the frontside guard and tackle are able to double team the #1 defender, the fullback should be able to break free into the crease repeatedly for long gainers (Diagram 6-47).

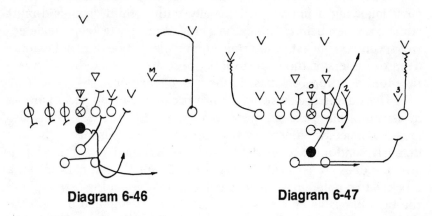

Diagram 6-46                    Diagram 6-47

## Wishbone Post Pass Versus Double Change-It (Invert)

Whenever the Wishbone faces two inverted safetymen adjusting their alignment to stop the Triple Option, the Post Pass is a natural play-pass call. There is no way the backside inverted safety can cover a properly executed post pass pattern. To put added pressure on the deep secondary defenders, the Wishbone Offense splits both ends wide to place added pressure on the safeties' wide alignments.

The play-action Triple Option fake helps to hold the defense long enough to break the post cut for the long bomb! The split end is coached to run straight upfield for eight to ten yards, then veer inside and look for the ball over his inside shoulder (Diagram 6-48).

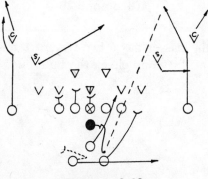

Diagram 6-48

## A Wishbone Drop-Back Passing Threat

There are situations when the Wishbone attack must resort to a
pass: following a fifteen yard penalty with a third-down-and-must
situation, when behind late in the game, or merely to keep the defensive secondary honest. The Triple Option play action does not fool the
deep defenders or the pass rushers; therefore, it is a definite advantage to use a drop-back pass in the above situations.

The quarterback's straight drop-back or back-up technique affords him a more panoramic view of the field. The defense is also
forced to place two defenders to cover both flats. This means that the
defensive end must cover the flat zone (Diagram 6-49). If the defensive end does not cover the flat, the passer hits the left halfback for a
quick flat completion. This means the defensive end is rushing, and
the tight offensive end is assigned to take a set step and pick up the
rushing defender ①. If the defensive right end is assigned to cover
the flat, the tight end takes his set step and runs a quick up route,
looking for the quick pass over his inside shoulder ②.

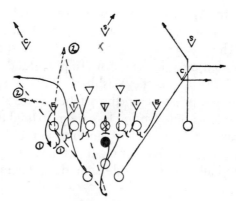

**Diagram 6-49**

Therefore, the passer has a two-way pattern—look for the left
halfback in the flat, first, and check the tight end, second.

# 7

# THE BREAK TWIN VEER OFFENSE

## How Will the Break Twin Veer Help You?

Since the Break Twin Veer features twins (wide slot) to one side of the formation and a split end to the opposite side, the opposition must stretch its defensive front. The two set offensive backs are split (break) and aligned behind their offensive tackles, which enables these backs to utilize their running and pass receiving specialties. Thus, this offensive formation gives the offensive unit a balanced running and passing attack.

The running attack emphasizes the Triple Option Veer series, the Pro Sweep, Twin Trap, and the Jet series. While many defensive coaches look at the Break Twin Veer Formation as primarily a passing formation, it is actually a strong running formation, as well.

The passing success from this offensive alignment may feature the dropback, sprint-out, play-action, or a combination of these passes. The three quick wide receivers plus the two set backs provide this offense with excellent passing potential (Diagram 7-1).

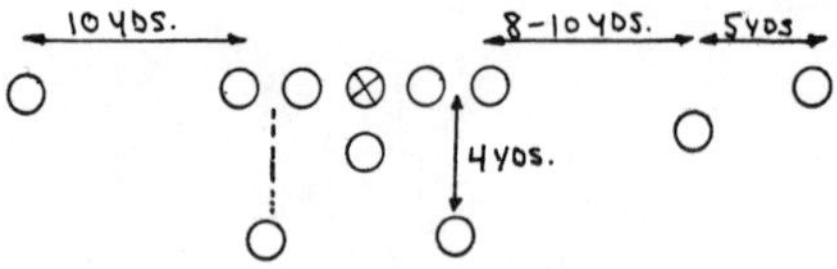

**Diagram 7-1**

## The Advantages of the Break Twin Veer

1. The two wide twin receivers have the ability to run their duo pass patterns.

2. These two wide-outs help to spread the defense, particularly the defensive secondary.

3. Three quick wide receivers are continual passing threats to break the game wide open.

4. The Triple Option attack is an excellent long-gaining threat to either wide-out side of the formation.

5. The alignment of five potential quick receivers offers the formation a balanced short and long passing game.

6. The width of the wide receivers forces the defense to spread out, leaving the defensive front vulnerable to quick offensive running threats.

7. This attack features the Triple Option pitch-outs, which are more successful to wide split-outs.

8. The pitch-outs, sweeps, and wide passing attack help to open up the quick-hitting Twin Trap Play.

9. The position of the wide-outs and their continual passing threats force the defensive secondary to defend in depth as well as width.

10. The Break Twin Veer Formation forces some defenders to line up in ineffectual walk-away alignments. The walk-away defender is considered a half man by the offense because he must defend against both the threats of the run and the pass.

## Requirements for
## the Break Twin Veer Personnel

*Three Wide Receivers*—The three wide receivers must be outstanding receivers with speed and superior moves. These three wide men must be able to execute the run-off block on deep secondary defenders.

*Two Running Backs*—These backs must be able to block to protect the passer and have the ability to come out of the offensive backfield and make the key catch. Both of these backs must have running ability to keep the defense balanced to stop the Twin Veer's pass-run threat.

*Quarterback*—A primary prerequisite for the signal caller must be a strong, accurate passing arm. The quarterback must be a good ball handler and an adequate runner to make the Veer Triple Option plays go.

*Center*—He must be able to make the one-on-one block to lead the running attack. The pivotman must also be an outstanding pass blocker to protect the all-important passer.

*Guards*—The guards must be able to lead the Pro Sweep and make the Twin Trap and Triple Option blocks. Like the center, the guards must be quick enough to pick up the pass rushers on a one-on-one pass protection block.

*Tackles*—The two anchors of the offensive line must be big and strong to make the post block and to help seal off the interior defenders on the Triple Option series. The tackles must be good, solid pass blockers with the ability to block the outside-rushing defensive ends or linebackers.

## The Break Veer Triple Option

When assigned to block the interior defenders, the offense is coached to leave two defenders on or near the line of scrimmage unblocked. The quarterback keys the #2 defender and places the ball into the dive back's pocket; if the #2 defender attacks the dive man, the quarterback disconnects and keeps the ball. The quarterback now keys the #3 defender. If the #3 defender attacks the quarterback, he

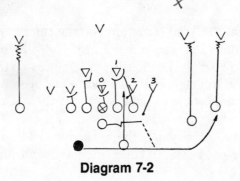

**Diagram 7-2**

is taught to complete the second phase of the Triple Option play by pitching the ball to the trailing back. If the #3 defender attempts to contain the pitchman by stepping across the line of scrimmage, the quarterback is forced to keep the ball and complete the third Triple Option phase by running his keeper play (Diagram 7-2).

This play is generally referred to as the Inside Triple Option play. Run from this two break back formation, it is commonly called the Veer Triple Option play.

There are many different methods of blocking for the Triple Option play. These methods are described in the next six sections.

## Interior Triple Option Blocking
## Against the 44 Defense

The basic Veer Triple Option blocking pattern utilized by the interior blockers versus the 44 Defense is illustrated in Diagram 7-3. The center takes a set step with his frontside foot to insure against a possible inside stunt by the #2 defender into the center-guard gap. The playside (right) offensive tackle uses a combo block with the offensive frontside guard. If the guard is able to block the #2 man by himself, the tackle goes to the second phase of his block and seals off the #1 linebacker.

**Diagram 7-3**

Against the "In" call (Diagram 7-4) the center and guard double team the #2 defender; the center's inside step helps out in this instance, while the frontside offensive tackle picks up the scrapping #1 linebacker. The frontside offensive tackle has been taught to look for the scrapping linebacker to show whenever the #2 man goes (stunts) away.

Against the "Out" stunt, the defensive tackle steps outside and the linebacker goes inside. The center and frontside guard double team the #1 linebacker, and the frontside tackle picks up the #2 man on a one-on-one block (Diagram 7-5).

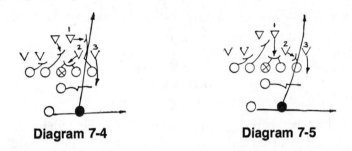

Diagram 7-4                     Diagram 7-5

Diagram 7-6 shows how to utilize a frontside and backside fold block to get good angles on the defensive tackles (#1 defenders) who may be angling toward flow. The offensive guards are both assigned to fold around their respective fire-out blocking partners. The fold blocker is coached to set block and fold around his partner. The fold blocker should place his right hand on his partner's inside hip and push the blocker to his assignment. This push serves two purposes— (1) it delays the step-around blocker long enough to clear the angle-back block of his partner and (2) it helps to pull the fold blocker around his partner's block and sets both offensive guards in the correct direction to cut off the defensive linebackers' pursuit courses.

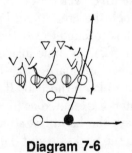

Diagram 7-6

## Interior Triple Option Blocking
## Versus the 52 Defense

Basically, the 44 Defense is blocked as shown in Diagram 7-7. The center blocks the #0 defender, getting his head between the #0

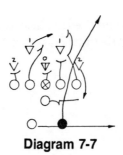

**Diagram 7-7**

man and the ball-carrying right dive back. The right guard blocks the #1 area and picks up the frontside #1 defender. The frontside tackle drives as if he is going to double team block the frontside #1 linebacker, but slides off this defender if it is apparent that the frontside offensive guard can block this defender by himself. If the #2 defender steps across the line of scrimmage, the quarterback hands the ball off to the right running back on the first phase of the Veer Triple Option.

Diagram 7-8 dramatizes an "X-stunt" between the frontside Oklahoma linebacker and defensive tackle. The #1 defender actually changes places (and assignments) with the #2 defender. The frontside guard steps forward with his inside foot and helps the frontside offensive tackle block the #2 defender who veers into the #1 defensive area. Meanwhile, the #1 linebacker scrapes off and heads for the #2 area. Once the frontside dive back observes the Veer path of the #2 defender, he cuts through the crease and looks to block the #1 defender. The quarterback is coached to key the #2 defender; as soon as the quarterback sees the #2 man angle inside of him, he immediately thinks "disconnect." Now the quarterback thinks "dive" unless the #3 defender forces him to keep the ball. If the #3 defender attacks the quarterback, the pitch is executed as illustrated in Diagram 7-8.

Diagram 7-9 displays the half blast stunt in which the frontside #1 linebacker blitzes to the backside and the #0 middle guard stunts

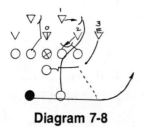

**Diagram 7-8**

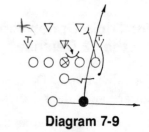

**Diagram 7-9**

toward the frontside #1 area. When this stunt takes place, the center sticks to the #1 man and the frontside offensive guard helps to double team the #0 defender. The frontside offensive tackle takes off in a direct route to block the frontside #1 defender; however, as soon as he goes away, the offensive tackle is coached to look for the backside linebacker scalloping toward him. As soon as the backside #1 defender shows, the frontside offensive tackle screens this defender's pursuit path. The backside guard shoots for the backside #1 defender and normally picks up the stunting frontside #1 defender. The backside offensive tackle blocks his normal #2 assignment.

## Interior Triple Option Blocking
## Against the 52 Gap Stack Defense

If the Oklahoma Defense uses a frontside middle gap stack, the center and frontside guard double team the #0 gap defender. The frontside offensive tackle blocks the #1 linebacker in an inside-stacked position. The backside offensive guard turns out on the backside #1 man, and the backside offensive tackle steps around, using an inside fold block, and blocks the #2 defender (Diagram 7-10).

If the defense lines up in a backside middle stack as illustrated in Diagram 7-11, the offense uses both a frontside and a backside fold block assignment. To the frontside, the tackle blocks the #1 defender

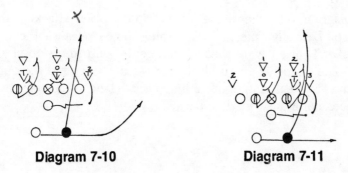

Diagram 7-10                    Diagram 7-11

while the guard steps around and fold blocks the #2 man. To the backside, the center blocks back on the backside #0 man, and the backside guard carries out his inside fold block assignment and picks off the backside #1 defender. When the #3 defender steps across the line, the quarterback hands the ball off to the diving back.

## Interior Triple Option Blocking
## Versus the 62 Defense

When attacking the 62 Defense, the Veer Triple Option offense must leave two defensive men free on or near the line of scrimmage. Therefore, both the #1 and #2 defenders must be blocked. This means the offensive guard and tackle must block the man over, while the center checks the frontside #1 linebacker to see if he is stunting to the inside. If he is not, the center is coached to block the backside linebacker's pursuit course. The quarterback gives the ball to the dive back as soon as the #3 man steps upfield to defend against the potential keeper play (Diagram 7-12).

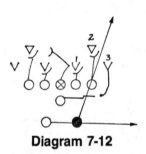

**Diagram 7-12**

## Interior Triple Option Blocking
## Versus the 61 Defense

Diagram 7-13 shows the Veer Triple Option attacking the 61 Defense. Basically, the give is a solid choice because the middle linebacker is often two-timed by the center and frontside offensive tackle. The offensive guard blocks the #1 defender and the quarterback gives to the diving right running back as long as the defensive #2 man does not attack the dive back.

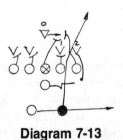

**Diagram 7-13**

## Interior Triple Option Blocking
## Versus the 53 Defense

Blocking the 53 Defense calls for the dive back to run a slightly wider crease. Now the dive back must cut off the outside hip of the frontside tackle's block. Since the offensive tackle has an advantageous angle on the #2 defender, the crease actually develops closer than it appears in Diagram 7-14. After the center cuts off the #0 man,

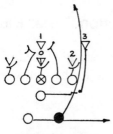

**Diagram 7-14**

the frontside guard blocks down on the stacked #1 linebacker. The frontside offensive tackle must be careful to cut off the #2 defender's penetration before trying to over-power the defender to the inside

## What Is the Outside Veer?

The Outside Veer is a Triple Option play, only it hits one hole wider than the normal Triple Option play. The quarterback still reads the Outside Veer and has his three options of the (1) dive, (2) keeper, or (3) pitch-out.

## Why Run the Outside Veer?

The Outside Veer play helps to make the normal Triple Option a more potent weapon. The offensive strategy behind utilizing the Outside Veer is that most defenses use a contain man to tackle the quarterback against the normal Triple Option play; if the defense plays the Outside Veer in the same manner, the dive man (back) will break free with no defenders assigned to stop him.

## Where to Run the Outside Veer

Run the Outside Veer to the tight end's side to use the power double team or co-op block. An excellent time to call this play is on the goal line, where the quarterback often breaks free for the score. The outside dive is normally successful against the 44 Defense. Against the normal seven man front, if the #3 defender tackles the dive back, the quarterback can execute a keep or pitch on the deep outside containing defender.

## The Outside Veer Option Power Block

Diagram 7-15 illustrates the Outside Veer Option versus the 52 Defense. Running this play to the frontside means that the quarter-

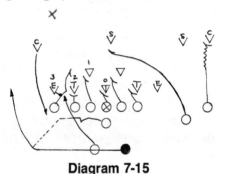

**Diagram 7-15**

back must read the #3 man (defensive end). If the #3 defender steps to the inside to stop the dive man, the quarterback pulls the ball out of the dive back's pocket and pitches or keeps reading the defensive assignment of the cornerback. In this diagram, the quarterback pitches the ball to the trailing back because the cornerback is attacking the ball handler.

## The Outside Veer Guard Pull

At times the Outside Veer play is called with the frontside guard pulling and sealing the backside pursuit just beyond the frontside offensive tackle's down block. Diagram 7-16 shows a down block by both the frontside offensive tackle and end, plus the pull by the frontside offensive guard. If the defensive end steps upfield, the quarterback is taught to hand the ball off to the dive back. The pulling frontside offensive guard is instructed to find the first opening beyond the offensive tackle's down block, then pull block back on the defensive pursuit.

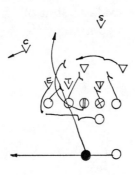

**Diagram 7-16**

If the defensive end shuffles to the inside and tackles the dive back, the quarterback is coached to disconnect and option off the next defender who shows. Diagram 7-17 shows the quarterback running the keeper because no one on the defense attacked him. Since the frontside blockers and the center have sealed off the defensive pursuit and the defensive end is protecting the outside versus the pitch-out, the defense gives the quarterback the Keeper Play.

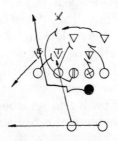

**Diagram 7-17**

## The Break Veer Cut Play

The Cut Play is a quick halfback slant play designed to take advantage of the bubbled, soft middle linebackers' defenses. Diagrams 7-18 and 7-19 show the cut maneuver against the 52 Bubble and 44 defenses. These defenses feature fast-flowing inside linebackers who are normally coached to scallop quickly to the outside and defend against the threat of the Triple Option sequence. Since this play starts out like the standard Triple Option play, the linebackers normally sprint to the outside to shut off the outside threat of the Triple Option's pitch or keep maneuvers.

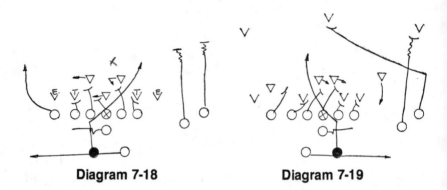

**Diagram 7-18**                    **Diagram 7-19**

A deeper mesh is emphasized for the quarterback, because the dive back needs as much time and room as possible to read the defense and make his cut. The ball carrier is instructed to "drive straight for the center's near foot, then make the cut for daylight." Normally, the coach should have the offense walk through this play versus the soft or bubbled middle defense. Once the dive back understands how the linebackers will react and how the interior offensive linemen will carry out their blocking assignments, he is better equipped to make an intelligent cut to daylight.

The Cut Play should not be run until the defense has been made to respect the threat of the Triple Option. Once this threat has been established, the Quick Cut will gain valuable yardage and help to hold the interior defense, enabling the Split Veer's Triple Option to achieve more outside success.

Against the hard-nosed 52 Defense, the dive back cuts in the opposite direction of the way the middle guard wants to go. The center is merely assigned to block the #0 defender. This means he blocks the middle guard any way the #0 man wants to go. Again, the quarterback makes the hand-off as deep as possible and continues down the line of scrimmage, emulating his Triple Option faking. Quick step-around or stunting middle guards play right into the scheme of the Cut Play (Diagram 7-20).

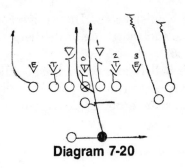

Diagram 7-20

## The Break Twin Veer Field Position Strategy

The quarterback is coached to watch the weak safetyman's position to determine which side of the offensive formation he should direct the offensive attack. Basically, the weak safetyman can only line up in three normal alignments versus the Break Twin Veer Formation. The defensive weak safetyman may line up in his (four) 4 position (directly over where the defensive #4 lineman would line up) in his normal four-across-the-board defensive secondary (Diagram 7-21). As long as the weakside safetyman is in his 4 position, the quarterback is instructed to direct his running and passing attack primarily to the twin slot side.

When the weakside safety lines up in his normal three deep (zero) 0 position (directly over the offensive center), the quarterback directs his attack depending on the field position (Diagram 7-22).

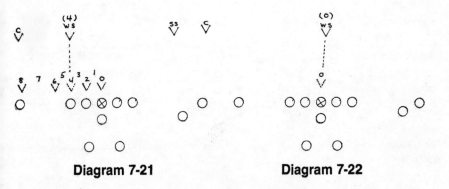

Diagram 7-21          Diagram 7-22

If the ball is on the offensive left hash mark and the safetyman is in his 0 position, the normal running and passing attack should be directed toward the twin slot side. The quarterback is also taught to run and pass some to the short side of the field to keep the defense honest (Diagram 7-23).

As soon as the ball is located in the middle of the field, the quarterback is instructed to run and pass basically to the split end's side, since the defensive secondary is overshifted toward the twin side (Diagram 7-24).

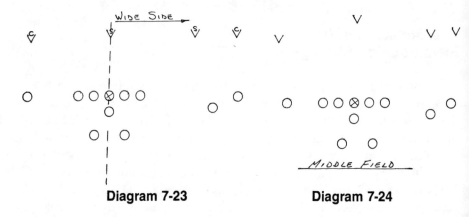

**Diagram 7-23**                    **Diagram 7-24**

The same offensive strategy is true whenever the twin wide receivers are to the short side of the field. The quarterback should direct his run-pass attack to the split end's side (Diagram 7-25).

Once the weakside safetyman moves his alignment all the way

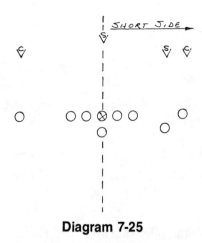

**Diagram 7-25**

across the midline of the offensive formation, the defensive secondary becomes overshifted. Now three of the defensive secondary players line up overshifted toward the twin slot side of the offensive formation. Since the safetyman lines up approximately over the guard-tackle gap, we refer to the safety as lining up in a 3 position. The overshifted safety's key alerts the quarterback to direct his offensive attack away from the twin slot set. From the safety's 3 position, it is impossible for the defensive safetyman to revolve to the single split end's side. This means the defensive cornerback is isolated on the weakside on a one-on-one pass coverage assignment (Diagram 7-26).

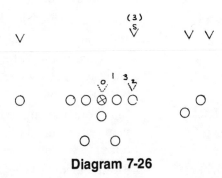

**Diagram 7-26**

The pass-run threat is prevalent to the formation's weakside (split end's side) regardless of whether the ball is placed in the middle of the field or on either hash mark.

## Pro Sweep

The Pro Sweep may be run with equal success from the Twin Veer Formation and the Pro Formation. Since the Pro Sweep helps to set up the following Twin Trap Play, these two plays should be run in sequence. Naturally, the bootleg passes are also part of the Pro Sweep and Twin Trap package.

The following Pro Sweep assignments are used against all defensive fronts. These assignments are:

Frontside Split End  —  Over, inside gap, linebacker
Frontside Slot End   —  Run-off technique

| | |
|---|---|
| Frontside Tackle | — Inside gap; if none, block #1 |
| Frontside Guard | — Pull right, gain depth, clear the end's block and kick out the first enemy outside our offensive end (if the end is split, the first defender outside the end's regular position). |
| Center | — #0; if none, reach block frontside |
| Backside Guard | — Inside gap; if none, pull right, turn up inside or outside of the end and seal inside. |
| Backside Tackle | — Cut off inside. |
| Backside End | — Sprint crossfield shallow |
| Quarterback | — Pivot and come back on a straight line from your center, hand off to the backside back, and continue your bootleg course. |
| Frontside Back | — Block outside kneecap of the first man on or outside the tackle; if none, first linebacker inside. |
| Backside Back | — Frontside step, receive ball from the quarterback, look up the block of the offensive end; give ground on third step; make your break off end's block. (Make sure you drive off your back foot). |
| Slotback | — *Frontside*—Drive off of line of scrimmage and take the man who is covering you. <br> — *Backside*—Run flag cut. |

## Pro Sweep Versus the 52 Gap Defense

The Pro Sweep is run away from the twins. Diagram 7-27 features a kick-out block on the cornerback while the frontside end blocks back on the #4 defender. The running back helps to set up this crack-back block by making a fake move toward the off tackle hole. Then the ball carrier breaks outside and cuts off the block of the pulling frontside offensive guard. The backside guard pulls and seals to the inside on the first pursuing defender who shows (Diagram 7-27). The Pro Sweep versus a three deep defense is discussed and illustrated in the next paragraph and diagram.

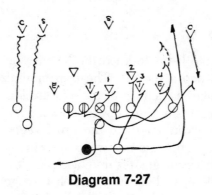

Diagram 7-27

## Pro Sweep Versus the 53 Defense

The Pro Sweep is often run to the twin side, especially to the short side of the field. If the defensive end (#4) lines up over the slotback, the slot man uses the frontside end's normal block and takes the defender any way he wants to go. The frontside offensive tackle and frontside back block the #3 and #2 defenders. The ball carrier then runs his sweep right up the passage between the frontside guard's turn-out block and the backside guard's seal-off block (Diagram 7-28).

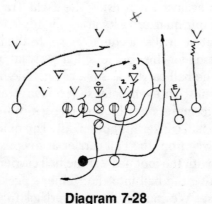

Diagram 7-28

(A comprehensive discussion and illustrations of the Pro Sweep may be found in Chapter 2.)

The success of the Pro Sweep helps to set up the Twin Trap Play. The Twin Trap is run off the same sequence as the Pro Sweep. Once the opposition has set up its defense to defend primarily against the sweep, the Twin Trap maneuver becomes a more consistent gainer.

## The Twin Trap

The Twin Trap helps to keep the defense honest and helps to make the Pro Sweep a success. The trap minimizes the defensive pursuit. It also takes advantage of the penetrating defenses and has proved to be a successful third down and long yardage play.

Actually, the Twin Trap and the Pro Sweep complement each other. The trap starts out like the sweep, only the ball carrier makes a quick cut off the backside guard's trap block and levels off or cuts back toward the goal line, picking up as much yardage as possible. The blocking assignments for the quarterback, slotback, center, backside guard, backside tackle, backside end, and frontside tackle resemble their initial movements and techniques on the Pro Sweep. Against certain defenses the frontside guard's path is similar to his Pro Sweep assignment.

The Twin Trap can only be as successful as the Pro Sweep, and vice versa. To make each play appear similar, teams may use the same formation whenever either play is called.

Usually the aggressive linemen or the defenders who are known to penetrate are the better targets for the trap; yet, previous experience has shown that the flowing or pursuing defenders are the easier defenders to run against when using the Twin Trap.

The path of our quarterback varies slightly with his path on the Pro Sweep in that he strikes a course closer to the ball carrier on the trap call. The reason for this course is that we want our quarterback to give the ball to the ball carrier as soon as possible because of a possible sharp cut against an even defense (no man is aligned nose-on to the center) and to make sure the quarterback can clear the running back to allow the ball carrier his option cut. The quarterback is taught to use the foot away from the ball carrier as his pivot foot, to make a 180 degree turn with the foot nearest the ball carrier. He should hand off the ball, looking the ball into the runner's pocket, then continue his bootleg course. We caution the quarterback to never glance back at the ball carrier but to watch how the defense plays the perimeter containment for a possible bootleg run or pass in future series.

The frontside or playside blocking back is taught to influence or run directly at the man on or outside of our offensive tackle. (The playside halfback may also be assigned to run in motion to influence the defender to be trapped). Then after the playside blocking back has influenced this defender, he is assigned to block the first man to the outside. The back's blocking technique is to employ a shoulder block on the defender, making sure he gains the correct inside-out angle on the defensive man. The blocking back is instructed that if he must lose the defender, he should make sure the defender takes the outside route around his head. The blocker should never lose the defender to the inside—he may slide off and tackle the ball carrier at the point of attack.

The ball carrier is coached to take a lead step, receive the ball from the quarterback, and direct his eyes on our pulling backside guard. The ball carrier must cut off the guard's trap block, then drive off his planted back foot and power into the trap hole like a fullback with the proper body lean and his legs chopping. He must be ready to be hit as soon as he reaches the trap hole.

The slotback to the playside is coached to drive off the line of scrimmage and crack back on the second deep defender. We want the slotback to cut down the defender from the blind side. He must make sure to get his head in front of his assigned defender. The slot man must take a route that will cut off the opponent where the defender will be rather than where he lines up. To accomplish the correct timing, we coach the slot man to drive off the line of scrimmage on a fly route, as if he were running a fly pass pattern. This helps to run off the deep outside defender. Then the slotback turns in on an angle for the deep back.

At times the ends simply use their regular run-off blocking techniques, depending on the given game. Both of our offensive ends may draw similar assignments, which are to sprint shallow across field and block the first opponent who shows. We assign the end toward the side of the flow to take the closest route to the line of scrimmage so that our two ends will not collide on their across-field assignments. The end to the side of flow is assigned the most shallow cut because we have found in the past that the defenders who run parallel to the path of the ball carrier are more of a threat than the defender from the opposite side who pursues on more of an angle. We instruct each downfield blocking end to get close enough to the defender so that he can step on the opponent's toes, then use the across-field blocking technique which calls for the blocker to aim at the secondary back's numbers. As soon as the end makes contact, he is taught to roll his hips and block through the opponent. The blocker then rolls after the man three times, taking away the defender's quickest pursuit angle.

## Twin Trap Versus the 62 Defense

When we attack the 62 Defense (Diagram 7-29), the point of attack is directly over our center's original position. The backside trapping guard pulls and kicks out the first man to show beyond the center. The defensive guard is influenced to the outside by both the offensive guard in front of him and the ball carrier. The frontside guard pulls to the outside, similar to the Pro Sweep, and has at least a mental, if not a physical, influence on the defender's urge to move with the frontside guard's action. The apparent wide flow of the ball carrier before his quick cut also brings about a tendency for the defender to protect to his outside, thus setting up the trap block.

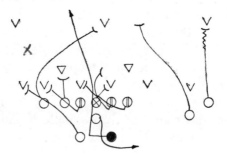

**Diagram 7-29**

Cutting off or sealing off defensive penetration is the assignment of the backside tackle. If no one penetrates, we want our pulling tackle to continue through the hole beyond our center's block and seal off any pursuing defenders. The right tackle must realize that he must not round the corner too wide so as to interfere with our ball carrier's path.

The center's backside assignment calls for a shoulder block on the defensive guard. He should fire out and get the biggest piece of the defender possible, working his block on an angle and always keeping his body between the defender and the ball carrier.

Our playside guard's technique helps to set up the man to be trapped. The defender lines up directly over our guard. The frontside guard pulls to his left and blocks the first linemen to his left and blocks the first lineman to his outside. The first part of this guard's blocking role is to block the man inside; if no man shows inside, he follows the above second section of his assignment.

The frontside tackle blocks the linebacker over him while our frontside blocking back turns outside on the first defender over or outside of our tackle.

Both of the ends carry out their normal assignments. The left end picks up the safety man on his shallow cut. The right offensive end blocks the cornerback using his regular run off blocking technique.

An across-field block by the left end eliminates the middle safetyman because he is on the backside.

The running back cuts off the hip of our trapper and breaks for daylight, taking advantage of his downfield blockers.

The quarterback should watch, not only the flow of the outside defensive perimeter on his bootleg route, but also the outside deep defender's reactions for a future bootleg pass in his area.

## Twin Trap Versus the Oklahoma Defense

Against the Oklahoma Defense (Diagram 7-30), we trap the defensive tackle who is set up for the trap block by our frontside blocking back. The blocking back's assignment is to execute an influence course on the tackle by running directly at the defender, then veering off and blocking the first defender to the outside. We feel that the frontside back's influence course holds the defensive tackle's attention long enough to set him up for our pulling guard's trap block. We are

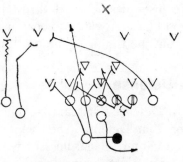

**Diagram 7-30**

sold on the fact that the defender who is to be trapped should be influenced from readying himself for the trap block.

Another method of influencing the defensive tackle, as well as the Oklahoma end, is to run the playside running back in motion to the outside and away from the point of attack. This motion may also influence the deep secondary defenders and cause them to rotate before the snap of the ball. With motion toward the twins, it may cause the defensive secondary to shift into a three deep situation, which is beneficial for our Pro Trap's downfield blocking assignments. Motion may also cause rapid movement by the linebackers to the offensive strength. This movement by the linebackers just before the center's snap often reduces their effectiveness because of the sudden movement and their foreign or new alignments.

Both offensive ends carry out their normal assignments while the playside tackle drives down on the Oklahoma linebacker. The frontside guard drives down on the middle defensive guard and the center has a fine angle block on the backside inside linebacker. The backside guard pulls and traps, and the backside offensive tackle pulls to seal off any defensive shooter. If the sealing tackle hears the defensive tackle's or any other pursuing defender's footsteps after he has pulled down the line, he has the option of quickly pivoting around and eliminating defenders with a powerful shoulder block. This reverse-action crack block usually limits the defenders' close pursuit of our pulling offensive linemen.

The slotback drives off the line of scrimmage straight downfield, then sprints to the inside, blocking the second inside defensive back.

The running back's route takes him through the fullback's original position, faking a potential wide sweep. The ball carrier cuts up through the hole at the last minute after timing our guard's trap block. The ball carrier must take a lead step and sprint parallel to the line of scrimmage, making his quick forward thrust just as the backside guard makes his trap block. A wide rainbow or curved route by our running back may ruin the timing of the pro trap maneuver.

## Trapping the 61 Defense

We block the 61 Defense (Diagram 7-31) in the same manner as we attack the 65 Goal Line Defense. The trapper blocks the first man to show beyond the center. Regardless of whether the defensive guards over the center pinch to the inside or veer inside, we still have the confidence that we can successfully trap this defense.

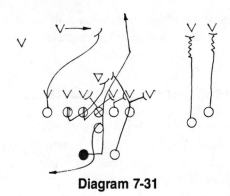

**Diagram 7-31**

The right guard helps to influence the defender to be trapped by taking a set step toward him with the inside foot. The right guard may be forced to make contact with the defender before he pushes off the inside foot and blocks outside on the defensive left tackle. Therefore, the right guard influences the defensive left guard in the same manner as the blocking back had set up the defensive tackle for a trap block versus the Oklahoma Defense as shown in Diagram 7-30.

The middle linebacker is blocked by the right tackle, who unloads on the linebacker just as our running back makes his cut at the point of attack. The right set back has an easy turn-out block on the defensive left end. The slotback's blocking rule is to crack back on the second deep back. We alert the slotback that he may be double covered at times and may have to fight himself clear of the defender who lines up over him. Fighting his way clear also includes employing several of the slotback's releases.

The left tackle pulls down the line of scrimmage in the same manner as our trapper and either cuts off the veering guard or clears our center's block and seals off all defensive flow going toward the point of attack.

The left end uses his regular across-field blocking techniques. If no defender shows immediately beyond the hole, the end should turn upfield and lead the ball carrier.

Using the right foot as a pivot, we want the quarterback to angle slightly back to the ball carrier to allow for our running back's sharp cut. The quarterback should continue his bootleg route, never glancing back at the ball carrier.

The ball carrier should take a lead step with his frontside foot and be ready to drive off his back foot quickly as the hole opens up over the center against the 61 Defense. Since there is a middle linebacker, the ball carrier must be ready to maneuver as soon as he reaches the hole, depending on the position of the middle linebacker at the time of the trap.

## Twin Trap Versus Short Yardage Defenses

We like to run the Twin Trap against the Gap Goal Line Front or short yardage defenses because of the fine angle blocks the center and trapper have. Another reason to select this play against the gap defense is that it is both a quick-hitting play and a trap. The striking quickness of the trap often makes it a long gainer against the short yardage defenses away from the goal line. Near the goal line, we tell our ball carrier to cut right off the trapper's tail, drop his shoulders, and be ready to drive like a fullback if the hole does not develop.

The right guard, right tackle, and right set back use turn-out blocks and make sure they never lose their man to the inside. We tell these blockers that if they ever have to lose the defender, make sure you lose him to the outside. By that time, the ball carrier will already have reached the point of attack. The left tackle pulls to his right with the foremost thought of cutting off the defender in the gap between the tackle and the pulling trap man. If the defender decides to pinch to the inside, the left tackle has to use a scramble block, going down on all fours and making sure his head is in front of the defender. The tackle cannot fall down; he must keep his feet and use his hands to maintain his balance. If the defender does not pinch, the tackle is coached to follow the pulling guard down the line, turning upfield just beyond the center's block. If the tackle goes beyond the center's block, he will get in the way of the ball carrier's path.

This is the ball carrier's sharpest cut because the defender whom we are trapping may be veering toward our center. Therefore, in all of the backfield play-timing practice sessions, we always use a guard or an extra back to pull and execute a trap on a dummy to emulate the Twin Trap. This technique is used to familiarize the ball carrier with both the short and long trapping techniques (Diagram 7-32).

The angle of our quarterback's path before the hand-off must be directed more toward the ball carrier's original position versus the Gap Eight Defense than any other, because we do not want our quarterback to force the ball carrier too wide beyond the hole.

*Coaching Point (Quarterback):* Keep the play timing sharp and do not force the ball carrier to round off the path or cut back into the hole (Diagram 7-33).

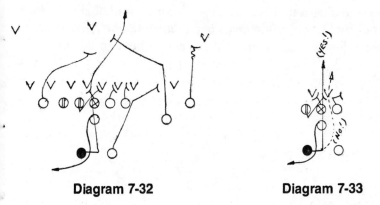

Diagram 7-32                                  Diagram 7-33

## The Twin Trap Against Five Man Front Defenses

With the more modern trend among the professionals, colleges, and high schools of using the five man front with six backs to minimize the success of the passing game, we feel the Pro Trap is a definite part of our wide-open attack. The trap should be an important part of every team's third down repertoire. The reasons we use the trap as an integral part of our quarterback's third down selection are:

1. Most defenses look for the wide sweep or pass.
2. Many teams insert an added defensive back to aid primarily in the pass defense rather than the run defense.
3. The five man front's main objective is to penetrate on third down.
4. The six defensive backs have a tendency to drop back quickly, thinking "pass."
5. The Twin Trap is run off a similar Pro Sweep play action and formation.

The offensive linemen should take their maximum splits against the five man front to isolate both the middle linebacker and middle guard and give these defenders a larger amount of defensive area to cover. This will give the running back a larger hole to cut through while the defensive tackle (whom we are trapping) is moved wider and becomes more susceptible to the pulling guard's trap block.

The center and right guard are able to double team the middle guard and are taught to drive the defender backward at about a forty-five degree angle. This angle helps to cut down the defensive pursuit. The right offensive tackle blocks down on the middle linebacker (Diagram 7-34).

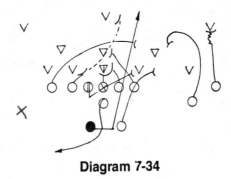

**Diagram 7-34**

The slotback curls back on the defensive end. We stress the importance of this downfield block because it puts the slot man between the defender and the ball carrier.

The left guard pulls and takes a good inside-out angle on the defensive left tackle. The trapper should execute his shoulder block to deliver a blow, then work his head to the outside, taking away the defensive tackle's quickest pursuit course. The left tackle pulls, following the guard's path, and swings around our double team block on the middle guard. The tackle then looks to the inside for a peel block. The left tackle has the authority to simply cut off the defensive right tackle if he believes this defender has a chance to cut off our running back before the ball carrier reaches the trap hole. We teach the tackle to keep his feet on all cut-off blocks.

The left end goes through his assigned across-field blocking patterns. The left end's across-field block is the most important because he is assigned to block the outside defensive left linebacker. The end must make a very shallow cut near the line of scrimmage because the linebacker will usually be working close to or on the line of scrimmage.

*Coaching Point*: If the ball carrier wants to take advantage of the left end's crossfield block, he should cut back after he sprints through the hole.

## Twin Trap Versus Gap Stack Defenses

Gap stack defenses have become more prominent each year because of the stemming and stunting possibilities of the linebackers stacked behind their linemen. Each year we put in more time blocking these gap stack looks.

Against the gap stack between the center and left guard (Diagram 7-35), we teach our center and right guard to block back across the hole while the left guard traps the lineman in the gap stack.

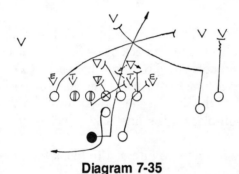

**Diagram 7-35**

Our right offensive tackle blocks the left linebacker wherever he goes. If the flow of the potential sweep pulls the linebacker over our tackle, we want our blocking tackle to use the shoulder block technique. After contact, we want the blocker to slide his head between the ball carrier and the defender. If the flow of our running back does not draw the linebacker away from the hole, we want the tackle to cut off the linebacker by using our scramble-block technique.

The trapper must be ready to trap the stacked left linebacker if he blitzes into our trapper's path. We teach our trapper to be aware of this possibility whenever he sees a gap stack.

Against the gap stack between the center and right guard, we again trap the lineman in the gap. The center blocks across the hole, picking up the first lineman to his left. The right guard uses a set step to influence the defender about to be trapped, then turns outside on the second defender to his right (Diagram 7-36).

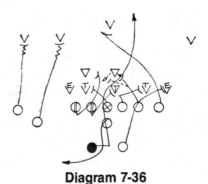

**Diagram 7-36**

The two key blocks which must be made are on the two lineback- ers. The left tackle executes a stack block in which he curls around our center's block and cuts down the right linebacker. On the other side, we assign our right tackle to block the left linebacker. He uses a shoulder block if the linebacker flows away from the hole, or a scrambling cut-off block if the linebacker decides to veer toward the hole.

We teach our offensive linemen to block the penetrating defen- sive linemen as shown in Diagram 7-37A.

In Diagram 7-37A, we trap the penetrating defense by having the center and the trapping left guard take a deeper angle on their blocks. We often find the linebackers looping either way whenever the stacked linemen penetrate into the gaps. Not only must the blockers be ready to take a deeper angle, but they should recognize that they must be quick, because the penetrating linemen are firing quickly into the gaps on all fours.

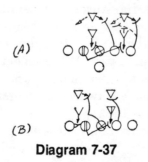

**Diagram 7-37**

We must be ready to switch blocks as demonstrated in Diagram 7-37B, because the left guard will be unable to use his stack block with the defensive tackle firing straight into his gap. Therefore, we coach the left tackle to cut or seal off the penetration and tell the center to alter his blocking course for the linebacker, since his original assigned defender has fired the gap. All we have done offensively is to exchange assignments between the guard and center.

The right guard fires straight at the stacked left linebacker. Since we are not sure whether the stacked linebacker will be blitzing, veering, or just reading and reacting to the flow of the ball carrier, we tell our blocking right guard to drive directly at his man and take the defender any way he wants to go. We know we cannot get offensive position to block him in a predetermined direction, so we just make contact with the defender and stick to him, driving him beyond the trap hole. The trapper must be ready to trap the stacked linebacker if he dogs into our trapping guard's area.

## Twin Trap Versus the 44 Defense

The Notre Dame or 44 Defense presents a number of looks because of its various alignments, stunts, and blitzes. While the eight man front usually presents a strong defense against the running attack, we have found that the Pro Trap often breaks the ball carrier loose for long runs against this even defense.

When attacking the 44 (Split Forty) look, we trap this defense in the same manner as we would block a gap look. We caution both our center and right guard to watch for possible straightforward gap blitzes by the two inside linebackers. The pulling guard must be ready to trap a pinching defensive tackle. Usually the defensive tackles line up pointing inside on a forty-five degree angle. These tackles are assigned to protect against the trap play and are coached to close down as soon as the guard crosses his face. Therefore, our trapping guards must be ready to root the defender out of his defensive position (Diagram 7-38).

When blocking the regular 44 Defense, we teach our center and right guard to block back on the twin inside linebackers, while our trapper blasts into the defensive tackle. The right tackle turns out on the left outside linebacker.

One of the most difficult blocks is the cut-off block by our left tackle. The difficulty of this block is increased by a pinching assign-

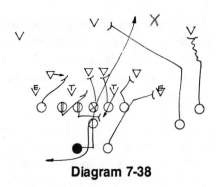

**Diagram 7-38**

ment of the defender. Therefore, the angle of our blocker's path is predicated upon the angle and quickness of the defender's move.

When the defense decides to use their double coverage assignment off the 44 Defense, we have to block a new defensive look. The double coverage middle look may resemble a 61 look as shown in Diagram 7-39. We like to put the defense in this look if we are having trouble cutting off the defensive right tackle as shown in Diagram 7-38. In Diagram 7-39, we have our center blocking back on the defensive right tackle, and our left tackle now employs his stack-block technique.

The 44 Defense also uses a double stack look with the double coverage adjustment to the flanker. In Diagram 7-40, we have a four-man wall set up which helps to seal off the backside pursuit. This wall helps to establish a path for the ball carrier to follow. We feel that once we break the runner through the trap hole, he should have an excellent chance to go all the way with this large amount of downfield blocking.

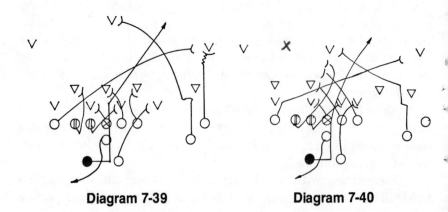

**Diagram 7-39**                              **Diagram 7-40**

Thus, we believe that the many 44 double coverage assignments by the defense help our offensive trapping game more than their defensive play.

## The Jet Series

The Jet Series features the quick pitch threat to turn the defensive corner. Off the Jet play sequence, the quarterback has the option of handing back to the trap, keeping the ball himself, or throwing the ball off the Jet's running fakes. The Jet Series gives the defense a completely different look from the Triple Option plays, the Outside Veer sequence, and the Pro Sweep/Twin Trap plays.

## Jet Motion Quick Pitch

Against an overshifted defense or the 52 Monster Defense, the Jet Quick Pitch is run with motion to the weak side of the defense (Diagram 7-41). The set right halfback goes in motion; as soon as he reaches the normal left halfback's original position, the quarterback begins his reverse pivot. As in the quick pitch to the strong side, the ball is pitched under the fullback's arms to the ball carrier, who is led downfield by the pulling frontside offensive tackle. The split end screen blocks the #3 defender and the diving fullback picks off the #2 man. This quick pitch to the weakside may also be executed by shifting the right set halfback to the left halfback's normal position.

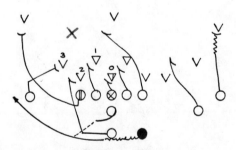

**Diagram 7-41**

## Jet Fake Pitch Trap

Many defenses favor an Eagle Defense against the constant threat of the Jet Quick Pitch (Diagram 7-42). To minimize the pursuit

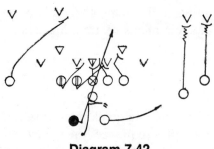

**Diagram 7-42**

of the Eagle linebackers, the Jet Fake Pitch Trap play is an integral part of this quick pitch offense.

The quarterback reverses out and makes a quick fake pitch to the right running back, who runs a wide pitch-out route. The left running back takes one step to his right, then sets a course directly over the right foot of the center. The ball carrier is coached to favor the double team block on the middle guard and to make his cut off the pulling guard's trap on the #1 defender. The quarterback steps back after the fake quick pitch and slips the ball off to the ball carrier with his right hand.

Diagram 7-43 features the Fake Pitch Trap against the even 62 Defense. The center blocks the backside #1 man and the left guard pulls and traps the frontside #1 defender. The most important coaching point of the trap versus the 62 Defense is for the ball carrier to make his cut directly off the tail of the trapper.

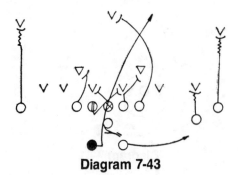

**Diagram 7-43**

*Coaching Point*: In the trap versus the 62 Defense, it is most important that the ball carrier cut directly off the tail of the trapping guard.

## Jet Quarterback Trap

Against the 62 Defense, a quick trap by the backside guard on the #1 man at the point of attack is the key on the Quarterback Trap Play. The quarterback fakes the quick pitch to the right halfback, right under the fullback's arms, then keeps the ball and makes his cut right off the tail of the trapper (Diagram 7-44). This play helps to keep the interior defenders honest and not "outside" conscious versus the Fullback Off Tackle and the Quick Pitch plays.

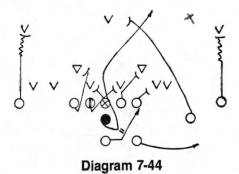

**Diagram 7-44**

## Jet Slot Counter

The Counter Play is run by the slotback who follows the trap block by the backside tackle (Diagram 7-45). The fullback's belly fake, coupled with the fake quick pitch, sets up the Counter Play. Although the Counter is only run two or three times a game, it has the big play potential.

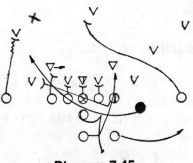

**Diagram 7-45**

## Jet Fake Trap Crosser Pass

The backfield action is similar to both the quick pitch and the quick pitch trap action, only the quarterback drops back and passes. The right tackle pulls and picks off the first rushing defender to his outside. The center blocks the #0 man and the other interior blockers block their normal drop-back pass protection assignments (Diagram 7-46).

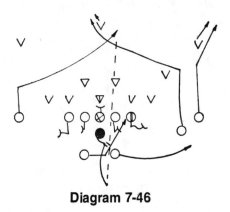

**Diagram 7-46**

Each potential pass receiver has a specific strategic assignment on this pass play. The right running back runs a flare pass pattern to entertain the Monster in the flat. A flag cut by the frontside split end takes the deep safetyman into the deep outside one-third zone. The slot man holds the middle safety in his middle one-third zone with a deep post cut. A seam cut is executed by the crossing left split end into the open area between the middle safety and the deep left safety. The quarterback delivers the ball as soon as the left split end clears the slotback's deep post cut.

## Slot Slant Pass Off Veer Action

Since a number of successful running plays are run off the Triple Option Veer series, the Veer-action passes are always solid play choices. The quarterback is taught to take two steps down the line of scrimmage and three steps back to set up in his passing pocket. The first two steps by the quarterback, the dive action by the frontside running back, and the pitch-out running route by the backside running back help to hold the frontside 52 Oklahoma inside linebacker.

These fakes help to free the slanting slotback into the underneath area between the two defensive safeties. The #0 position of the middle safetyman gives the slanting receiver a larger-than-normal crease in which to catch the football (Diagram 7-47).

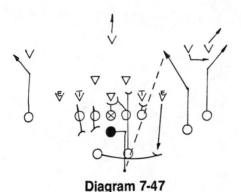

**Diagram 7-47**

## Reading the Secondary Pass Coverage

Some professional teams and many passing college teams have given up the difficult task of reading the pass defense's coverages. Since many pass defenses have become so complicated and so well-coached, it is very difficult for some quarterbacks to intelligently read the deep secondary defenders. Therefore, many coaches have assigned a primary pass receiver and a secondary or lay-off pass receiver. This means the passer will pinpoint one specific receiver and have only one secondary receiver to throw to if his primary receiver is not open.

Some coaches have predetermined a specific pass cut for both the primary and secondary receivers, while other offenses allow the receiver to determine his pass route depending on the movement of the pass defense or a particular pass defender. Regardless of how the coach teaches his passer or receiver to read the pass defense, each year it is becoming more difficult for the passer to read the pass coverage.

## Swing Pass

Against the three deep, locked-in secondary defense, the Swing Pass away from the Twin Slot side is often open. If the frontside outside linebacker attempts to pick up the swinging receiver on a man-to-man assignment, the passer holds the ball a moment longer and throws it downfield, about ten yards deep. This forces the outside linebacker to run with a sprinting running back, which is a most difficult assignment for most big linebackers to accomplish (Diagram 7-48).

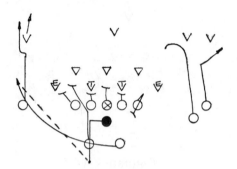

**Diagram 7-48**

Thus, the primary receiver is the swinging running back and the secondary receiver is the curling slotback. The slotback becomes free whenever the defensive secondary attempts to roll to the play-action side of the offensive formation. This means the right cornerback is assigned to the flat, the middle safety takes the deep outside one-third area, and the strong safety covers the deep one-third middle zone (Diagram 7-49).

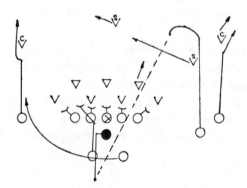

**Diagram 7-49**

The Throw-Back Curl Pass must be aimed directly for the slot-back's numbers so the receiver can position his body between the ball and the deep secondary pass defenders. The curling slotback is coached to slide into the open area so the passer is able to throw the ball between the linebackers rather than over the underneath pass defenders.

## Backside Back's Read Pass

Another strategically successful pass of the Break Twin Veer Formation is the Backside Back's Read Pass. The quarterback starts down the line for two steps (faking his normal Triple Option play), then drops straight back for three steps. The backside running back runs off the corner and reads the movement of the weakside safety-man if the defender is in his 4 position. If the weakside safety drops back into his deep middle one-third coverage, the back runs his (1) flat route. If the weak safety breaks for his deep outside one-third zone, the running back reads this defensive move and runs an arrow route directly at the weakside safety's original position (2) (Diagram 7-50).

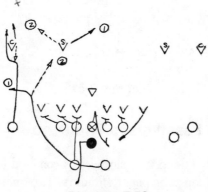

**Diagram 7-50**

Therefore, the primary receiver is the backside running back and the secondary receiver is the left split end. The left split end runs a fly pass pattern; the quarterback throws to this secondary receiver if the right cornerback rolls up into the flat and the weakside safetyman attempts to cover the deep outside one-third zone.

## Veer Tight Pass

The Tight Pass is thrown off the normal Veer-action series. This is an option pass route for the tight end. The tight end runs three steps to the outside, then turns upfield. A sideline cut is (1) executed by the tight end if the strongside safety drops backwards; if the strong safety runs an inverted route, (2) the tight end is coached to continue his pattern straight upfield and catch the ball on a fly route over his inside shoulder. The split end and flanker run pass patterns to keep the deep defenders occupied or away from the primary receiver.

A two-step veer fake is executed by the quarterback, who then drops straight back three steps and passes to the tight end. The dive back picks up the #1 defender while the backside running back blocks the #3 man. (Diagram 7-51).

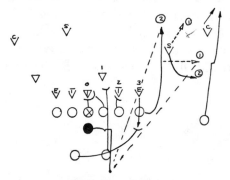

**Diagram 7-51**

## Veer Slot Deep Pass Versus Two Deep

Against the two deep, the slotback is coached to run a deep cut and split the two deep zone pass defenders. The quarterback fakes his normal Veer action and throws deep to the slotback over the middle (Diagram 7-52). There is no specified depth in which to hit the slot receiver; it depends on the depth the linebackers drop and how quickly the slotback gets open. The passer is coached to hit the receiver as quickly as possible and let the slotback run for yardage.

The passer takes his first two steps to fake the normal Veer dive, then retreats straight back three steps and hits his target.

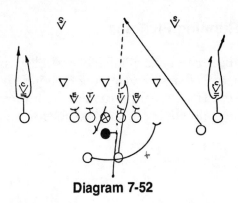

**Diagram 7-52**

## Drop-Back Shuffle Pass

The Shuffle Pass (Diagram 7-53) is particularly effective to the weakside of the Twin Formation. The left split end runs his flat pass pattern and the weakside running back is assigned to run a flare to decoy the 52 linebacker to the outside. The turn-out block by the weakside tackle, plus the weakside guard's and center's double team block on the middle guard, opens up a big hole for the strongside running back's shuffle pass.

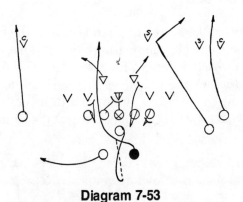

**Diagram 7-53**

The quarterback drops straight back, as he normally does when he executes a drop-back pass; then, he shuffles an underhand pass to the running back. The passer tries to hit the receiver in the stomach area with an easy underhand throw.

## Drop-Back Running Fly Pass

The drop-back pass has a number of possible pass routes. Against the three deep, locked-in secondary, the Running Fly Pass is a potential gamebreaker. The strongside running back runs a deep fly pass pattern into the crease between the two defensive safeties (Diagram 7-54).

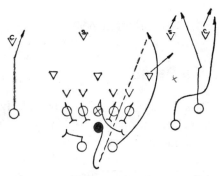

**Diagram 7-54**

## Bootleg Flood Pass

A double dive fake by the quarterback, plus the bootleg action, helps to free the frontside running back into the flat area (Diagram 7-55). The quarterback makes a quick token fake to the backside dive back. The quarterback then bootlegs the ball back toward the twin slot side, following the backside pulling guard. It is the responsibility of the passer to make a strong running threat at the corner to help lure

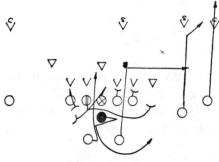

**Diagram 7-55**

one of the deep secondary pass defenders to commit himself to the running bootleg threat of the quarterback. The strong flood pass route of the play helps to free the set back into the flat area. If the corner-back rolls into the flat area or the safetyman inverts into the flat area, the slotback is normally free running his twelve yard deep sideline pass pattern.

## Halfback Throwback Pass

Against the 44 Defense, the Slot Formation tries to hit the seams in the three deep secondary. Normally, the three deep middle safety man will key the direction of the quarterback's sprint or roll action. In Diagram 7-56, the quarterback dispatches all five of his receivers and sprints to his right. The quarterback pulls up and throws back to his backside halfback, who runs a fly-seam pass pattern. Since the middle safety has been pulled out of position, the throwback pass is open.

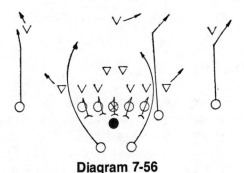

**Diagram 7-56**

# INDEX

# A

# B

# C